VIVA LOFTON

MEMOIR OF A BEGINNER DAD

LONNIE LAZAR

NASCAR® is a registered trademark of National Association for Stock Car Auto Racing, Inc.

"Save Yourself"
Words and Music by Lonnie Lazar
© 1999 by Lonnie Lazar

"I Know What Love Is"
Words and Music by Lonnie Lazar
© 2000 by Lonnie Lazar

"Up By My Place"
Words and Music by Lonnie Lazar
© 1999 by Lonnie Lazar

Every reasonable effort has been made to trace copyright holders of material reproduced or referenced in this book, but if any have been inadvertently overlooked the publisher would be glad to hear from them.

All photographs in this book are copyright protected and used by permission.

LIBRARY OF CONGRESS CATALOGUING-IN-PUBLICATION DATA

Lazar, Lonnie, 1960– author.

ISBN: 979-8-9922567-0-3 (sc)
ISBN: 979-8-9922567-1-0 (hc)
ISBN: 979-8-9922567-2-7 (e)

Viva! Lofton: Memoir of a Beginner Dad / Lonnie Lazar. –2d U.S. edition.
1.   Subject Matter–Memoir.   2.   Social Matter–Opinion.   1.   Title.
2d U.S. Edition 2024

LONBUD MEDIA LLC

1 3 5 7 9 10 8 6 4 2

For the child in you

Gate gate paragate parasamgate bodhi svaha
Go, go.
Go beyond.
Go completely beyond and rest in your true nature.
– From *The Heart Sutra*

You do not have to be good.
You do not have to walk on your knees

for a hundred miles through the desert repenting. You only
have to let the soft animal of your body love what it loves.

Tell me about despair, yours, and I will tell you mine.
Meanwhile the world goes on.
Meanwhile the sun and the clear pebbles of the
rain are moving across the landscapes,

over the prairies and the deep trees, the mountains and the
rivers. Meanwhile the wild geese, high in the clean blue air,
are heading home again.

Whoever you are, no matter how lonely, the
world offers itself to your imagination,

calls to you like the wild geese, harsh and exciting—

over and over announcing your place

in the family of things.

Wild Geese
Mary Oliver (1935-2019)

CONTENTS

Preface..ix

Part 1: People Get Ready 1

September 16, 1999—San Francisco 3

Ten Things About Me You May Not Know 6

El Jefe...9

My Mother's Tale – Part 1 14

My Mother's Tale – Part 2 21

Who Are You?...26

These Are My People 31

October 6, 1999—San Francisco 39

All Down The Line: A Favor for Keith Richards 40

In The Voodoo Lounge..47

Save Yourself...54

Running Down a Dream 55

November 14, 1999...63

November 20, 1999...67

December 15, 1999 69

December 29, 1999—Jaèn, Spain....................................72

The Year 2000 78

I Know What Love Is 88

Part 2: Viva! Lofton..89

June 13, 2000 91

July 23 93

July 29 94

October 29 95

December 25..97

2001..98

September 11, 2001..109

October 10, 2001—San Francisco 114

October 16... 117

November 25 120

A Side Note on Football Sundays, Justice, and
    Where You Spend Your Personal Energy.................................122

December 16...125

December 30...129

2002..130

The Bridge: Boomers, a Millennial, and The Family Bed 137

1986: Detained in China 143

2003.. 161

Part 3: I Just Have To Say... **169**

The Blogging Years: 2003 – 2008 171

2004..177

2005..190

2006..197

2007.. 209

2008..216

Part 4: Open Salon.. **221**

Blogging at Open Salon: 2008 – 2009.. 223

There's Always Been Ethel... 225

The Boys of Summer..231

I Feel the Earth Move 232

Burning Down the House...235

Don't Just Sit There, Do Something.. 238

The Death of Hope 241

I Have Big News To Share 244

Defining Moments 247

Part 5: And Then It Was **251**
May 27, 2014 253
2020..265
Flashback: April 17, 2018 276

Epilogue 277
Acknowledgments...281
About the Author..285

PREFACE

"What we've got here is ... failure to communicate."

Such is the iconic line Strother Martin delivers in the classic movie, *Cool Hand Luke*, when Paul Newman, playing the film's title character, makes a smart-aleck remark, refusing to conform to the behavioral norms of the rural southern chain gang he finds himself sentenced to for petty crimes and drunkenness.

Martin plays "Captain," the prison warden who beats Luke like a dog for his insolence and uncooperative ways. He delivers the line in a deliciously seething, sadistic tone, emphasizing the vowel sounds in *failure* and *communicate* to immortalize that snippet of film to nearly every generation of American boys and men alive between the film's release in 1967 and Newman's death in 2008.

Have you seen *Cool Hand Luke*? A viewing provides riveting, powerful insight to the character, motivations, and flaws of certain archetypes of the American male, casting in stark relief the brutal, immoral, authoritarian nature of our prison system.

The archetype for which Newman's portrayal earned him a Best Actor Oscar nomination, is a laconic, good looking, independent-minded person, one with an easy sense of good-hearted, playful humor, who is yet stubborn, hard-headed and unwilling—perhaps unable—to respect the often-arbitrary demands of authority.

As a teen struggling with my own relationship to authority—parental, educational, and social—a favorite uncle bestowed upon me the nickname "Luke." He did so in homage to Newman's character, after some run-in or another I'd had with his cousin, my father, who, like Captain in the film, felt driven to employ ever-more-draconian punishments upon me in his efforts to have me toe the line. I admired Newman, the actor, and could totally relate to Luke, the character, so I embraced the nickname, feeling seen and understood by my uncle in ways I felt my father couldn't, or just didn't, see or understand me.

The 1960s and 70s were a transitional time for norms around the acceptable treatment of children. I recall being as young as four or five, forced to go outside into the yard to pick out a "switch" with which my mother (at that age) would, sometimes lightly, sometimes less-so, whack the backs of my bare legs for having failed to mind my behavior.

As I grew older, my father took up the reins of corporal punishment and I remember, at ten or eleven, his beating me on occasion with a length of plastic track from a *Hot Wheels* race car set, at least one time so vigorously it left not just welts, but bleeding grooves on my lily-white bottom.

Still later, in my sophomore or junior year of high school, I had to bend over in a private office, to grab my ankles and count—one, sir...two, sir...three, sir—while the vice-principal struck me ten times on my ass with a thick wooden paddle.

When I was eighteen or nineteen, my attitude and behavior once so enraged my father he was unable to restrain himself from punching me in the jaw with a closed fist.

Looking back, I ask myself if I deserved that kind of treatment and the answer is, of course, *No*.

In the vast majority of instances, my transgressions had been, like Luke's, a failure to *behave*. Yes, sometimes I'd lied. Others, I'd stolen. A few times, I'd injured someone, or destroyed property. But did a beating ever make me change my behavior? Did it get me to behave, or cause me to respect authority? Like Luke, it did not.

Fortunately, unlike the tragic film character, my eventual brief and limited encounters with the American criminal justice system never landed me on a chain gang breaking rocks in the hot sun. In time, I became able to express my individuality and remain aloof to authority in ways that didn't get me beaten or detained (too often) against my will.

I believe I remain, at 60, as laconic, good-looking, and independent a man as the 14 year-old who earned the nickname Luke, though the story you're about to read has its own sad and tragic elements.

What we've got here may yet prove a failure to fully communicate the character, motivations, and flaws of its author, but this collection of writings, produced over a period of more than twenty years, is my attempt to leave (at least) an honest (if incomplete) record of thoughts, beliefs, observations, and questions about the nature of manhood, of fatherhood, of childhood, partnership, citizenship—and of what it means, to me, to be human: to be flawed and tragic; to be good-hearted and playful and hard-headed.

While Captain's line in *Cool Hand Luke* may be that movie's most iconic, Luke's friend Dragline, played by George Kennedy (another Hollywood great, who won a Best Supporting Actor Oscar for his role as the prison gang leader who first tries to break Luke and then comes to admire him, along with the rest of the prisoners, for his *refusal* to be broken) has the line that speaks to me, telling Luke: "You're an *original*, that's what you are!"

PART 1

PEOPLE GET READY

SEPTEMBER 16, 1999—SAN FRANCISCO

I conceived, initially, of a journal, a diary of sorts, so that someday my child might have an idea of what was going on, what I was doing, thinking, wanting, wishing, and planning prior to his/ her/its arrival. I hoped the writing might one day be helpful in untangling a host of inscrutabilities.

Hey, you. I don't know what to call you yet, because as I write this, you are just a tiny bunch of cells growing in your mother's body. We saw you on an ultrasound monitor for the first time today—saw your little heart beating and your little body starting to form in your mother's uterus—and I thought it might be time for me to start trying to explain a few things, to start trying to tell you how I feel, to put down in words some things I'd like you to know. I have actually been talking to you for about half your "life" already. The doctors say you are seven-and-a-half weeks old, but by my count it's only six-and-a-half. Either way, for the past three weeks, since we've known you were there, I've been asking you to grow, and be strong and healthy, and to come to us when you are ready.[1] I get down on my knees in the

---

[1]   Right off the bat, we encounter one of the great controversies of our time: When does "life" begin? The corollary, of course, includes the controversy around abortion, whether and when it should be legal to willfully terminate a pregnancy; whether and if doing so ought to be considered "taking a life," or, more colloquially, "murder." Obviously, I'm talking to a zygote, not even yet a fetus, and so, clearly, in this particular case, I reveal a belief that "life" begins before birth. I also want to make clear, however, my belief that answers to questions around these controversies, for any particular person or set of parents, are 100% personal and ought to be completely the province of personal decisions made in consultation with medical and spiritual advisors. I do not believe there is, nor ought there be legal or political components to the answers.

3

kitchen sometimes in the morning and I put my mouth right up to your mother's stomach and say, "Good morning, little baby; come to Papa!"

It's pretty silly, I know, but I've been imagining you for over twenty years and by now I don't really care how silly I look or seem, I just want you to come and join our little party.

Your mother and I are both so excited about you. We've experienced two or three miscarriages over the past several years, losing pregnancies at and before the stage you are in now, and we've had difficulty getting pregnant at all lately, so the fact you seem to be on the way has us both very, very happy; also nervous, excited, and scared, all at the same time.

We both worry about whether you will be born in good health, like all parents do, I'm sure, before their children come into this world. And I worry, too, about what it will be like for you here, how we will seem to you, whether I can be as good a father and a friend to you as I have always imagined myself and want to be.

I know (at least I believe)[2] you have chosen me, chosen us, as your parents to bring your spirit back into a world you have seen before, and I want you to know I feel honored and blessed. I hope I can be everything you want and need me to be on your journey back to the place we all come from.

Besides trying to come up with the right name for you and praying for your safe journey here, we are consumed with trying to buy the house you'll be living in when you first arrive. We've been living here for seven years, renting it from our landlord, who told us a month ago he will sell the building.

---

[2] My beliefs are hard-won, having been raised in a Jewish household, educated in Christian schools, and influenced by my own investigations and observations, which led me to embrace an understanding largely aligned with that described by Siddartha Gotama, the historical Buddha. Please read *Siddartha*, by Herman Hesse, to learn more.

San Francisco is one of the most expensive places to live in the world and we were not prepared to go out and find another place to live right now, so we are trying to figure out how to buy this place from him.

Another big thing in our lives at the moment is the New Years celebration we'll be attending soon in Spain. Friends and I have been planning it for two years. The calendar is turning from 1999 to 2000. We've got about sixty people coming from the US, Canada, and Europe to meet at a castle in the southern town of Jaèn for five days. I imagine you'll hear stories about it, but we've still got logistics to work out and making it a successful event weighs on my mind.

This is also the beginning of football season, though sports purists would say baseball's pennant races should be the focus of the sporting world until after the World Series. I guess it depends on what sport you like best. Football was always very big in the South, where I grew up. I'm a big fan of the Green Bay Packers, so I get pretty excited when football season starts. I'm pretty well only concerned with the fate of the team from the land of cheese on Sundays between September and January. This year, however, my favorite baseball team, the New York Mets, has a good squad. They look to be in the hunt for the World Series, so I'll be paying attention to baseball too in the next six weeks or so.

That's about all for now, little one. It's late and your mom, who works nights out at the airport, will be home soon. I'm going to go get in bed to warm it up for her and wait for her to bring you home. I'll try to write often and give you updates on what is going on with us and with this crazy, wonderful, exciting, scary, mixed-up, amazing world. I'm not 100% convinced I'm doing a responsible thing bringing you into it, but in my heart and in my spirit I have lots of love and optimism. I believe everything happens for the best. And so I say again, "Come to Papa!"

TEN THINGS ABOUT ME YOU MAY NOT KNOW

I wrote the following introductory piece as a meme exercise in an online social media journal known as "Open Salon" in 2008. Writings from that journal are featured further along in this book but here s a peek at how the guy who wrote it saw himself at the time.[3]

1. **I am good.**

   Throughout my childhood and well into adulthood I was bombarded with the charge of being *bad* (my own parents in the angry, torch-bearing mob), but I always believed in my heart's essential goodness. After years of therapy, yoga, and meditation, my belief is solid and luminous as the rock at Kyaktiyo, in Burma.

2. **Babies (with scant ability to focus a few centimeters beyond their retinas) see me.**

   Ninety-eight percent of them smile. I believe this confirms the truth of #1, though some say it could be gas. I pretend the two percent who cry are overcome by the enormity of my goodness.

3. **I am not afraid of dying.**

   One afternoon in 1986, I sat exhausted by an acute case of giardia, nearly immobilized by sciatica, in a light snowfall on top of a ridge behind Drepung Monastery in Tibet. I watched a young Tibetan

---

[3] *Open Salon* (public life July 28, 2008-March 31, 2015) was, according to Wikipedia, "a hybrid blogging platform and social network site started by the Salon Media Group, Inc. According to Salon Editor-in-Chief Joan Walsh, "Open Salon gets rid of traditional gatekeepers, and makes our smart, creative audience full partners in Salon's publishing future." (Joan might describe it a bit differently in private.) An active commenter at the flagship site, I began writing at *Open* before the public beta.

boy, his father, and the father's father ascend the steep ridge to perform an ancient ritual in honor of their ancestors. They barely acknowledged my presence beyond offering a taste of the rough barley gruel used in their ceremony. The skies opened and the bright sun that shines so only on the Roof of the World bathed our ridge-top and the valley beyond in clear light. A sense of painless freedom and an understanding that death is a gateway on the journey home filled my being.

4. **Cooking is a passion; eating, a vice.**

My heaven is filled with fresh organic produce, sharp knives, and lots of counter space. I cannot say no. To me, the purest expression of love is a well-prepared meal.

5. **My lovers come first.**

We come together more often and stay together longer. I remain friends with my high-school sweetheart and lived with my first and only wife for twenty years.

6. **If Sally's feet[4] are really as beautiful as she describes them, I would like to suck her toes.**

(OK, that could be red-lining the TMI meter.)

7. **My son has me worried.[5]**

He is just like me and I grieve for his heart under the onslaught of repression and negativity that may be headed his way. Whenever we got his in-vitro ultrasounds, all of the OB-GYN nurses exchanged knowing looks, discussing his heart rate. I was, like, "What? What?" And they were, like, "Oh it's nothing to worry about, he's got a very strong heart." I wouldn't have it any other way, actually, but I still worry for him.

---

[4]   You'd like to know, I'm sure.

[5]   Reader, be not confused. Recall this list was compiled well after his birth and is placed here only to give you (and him) insight into just who the hell the author thinks he is.

8. I can keep a secret.

I am the proverbial hole-in-the-ground to whom you can tell something you promised someone you'd never tell anyone but which you've got to tell someone, or else you're just going to die. I'd prefer you kept it to yourself, but if you must, your secret is safe with me.

9. I majored in English in college.[6]

Samuel Taylor Coleridge and William Blake are my heroes, but John Donne was my inspiration. In my sophomore year I tried to woo a beautiful Jersey girl I had a crush on by composing an ode to her vagina in the style of Donne's ecstatic poetry. She didn't get it. I have nonetheless continued to plumb the line between ecstasies of the flesh and those of the spirit.

10. For thirteen years, I ran a wildly successful, iconic dance club in San Francisco's Lower Haight.

In a 1992 feature on "places to be" in New York, Los Angeles, and San Francisco, *Details* magazine said my club was where you wanted to be at midnight on a Saturday night. Today, I am broke as fuck and looking for work.

And yet, it's a wonderful life.

---

[6] The most enlightening and transformative undergraduate classes I took were those with Professor Purvis Boyette at Tulane University in New Orleans. I was just twenty and while I had already set a course of independence and exploration, I did not yet understand the intellectual and artistic traditions from which I'd grown. The class I recall being most influential was "The Poetics of Ecstasy." *Wild Poets of Ecstasy*, a more recent anthology that includes many of the works I studied then says, "So what is the core experience? *Ekstasis* is a Greek word that means to stand (*stasis*) outside (*ek*) of oneself. Its opposite is *enstasis*, or to remain fixed within oneself. It is possible to experience *ekstasis* in a variety of emotional states...[from being] 'swallowed in a sea of grief'... to being 'beside myself with anger.' *Ekstasis* can be present in any moment in which [we perceive things] contrary to our self-definitions ... As a term, however, ecstasy has evolved to signify a more positive experience, one accompanied by or followed by such feelings as joy, bliss, rapture, euphoria, or any intense positive emotion." I have been seeking opportunities to stand outside myself and experience intense positive emotions my entire adult life.

EL JEFE

Before we further introduce the person for whom this project was conceived, whose impending arrival inspired my earliest efforts at putting into words what it meant to me to be about to behold for the first time a human being produced from my own flesh and blood, the reader should understand a bit about the people who had a hand in producing the author himself. And because, in many ways this is a story of fathers and sons and a story about boys and men, let us begin with The Chief.

My own father was called many things by many people in his life. But I and my friends, once we became teenagers and found the temerity to approach him on what we fancied was something like equal footing, called him "The Chief." In reality, he and his accomplishments towered over us, despite the fact he was well under six feet tall. He had a presence—magnetism—and a zest for life that filled every space he occupied; not in a showy way that caused him to be the center of attention, but rather with confidence and gravitas, and a wealth of experience that made him the embodiment of authority.

He was a mostly evenings-and-weekends father when I was a child because he was in sales. He owned his own wine and liquor distributorship, but he was also its hardest working and best salesman. When I grew older and got to observe him in settings beyond our home, where everyone under his roof lived under his rules, or in the file-jammed office from which he issued edicts and commands related to his business, I saw he could talk anyone into buying whatever he was selling. This inborn talent made him a wildly successful fundraiser for charitable causes and the arts in the community where we lived. It allowed him to get legislation passed at local and state levels without ever holding political office. And it allowed him to get me out of all manner of difficulties with my schools and, later, with the law, in my wild and profligate youth.

For a time I thought I might be like him. I tried to follow in his footsteps, but all I ever managed was an ability to enjoy the fine things in life that his unflagging determination and natural salesmanship won him—which he shared with me. I reveled in the glow of being at his side in the best hotels and the finest dining rooms, in the best seats in the house at Super Bowls, Kentucky Derbys, US Opens, and heavyweight title fights. I loved when he'd regale me with tales of his own youth, of living in Miami before getting his start in the liquor business, of hustling with his brother selling Johnson's Baby Aspirin as "hurricane pills" to Blacks in Liberty City when storms rolled up.

I imagined the glamorous life he led as an investor in racehorses, known by name to all the porters in the clubhouse at Hialeah Park; as a nightclub owner and talent manager to comedians Slappy White and Redd Foxx; as a friend and running buddy to Joe DiMaggio, and to reputed mobsters Jimmy Blue Eyes and Meyer Lansky.

When I was old enough to hear the unfiltered stories, he told me of the pre-Castro days in Havana, of taking speed boats across the Florida Straits to spend days at a time there gambling in the casinos, or shacked up in a hotel room, only ever calling the front desk for more ice, fresh towels, and another pair of hookers. He told me he felt the world change the night he dined at a raucous samba club in Havana, when Castro's men came in and shot Batista's Chief of Police at the next table.

The punk antics of my own youth seem pale imitations of The Chief's wild ride, as do the not-inconsiderable successes of my professional and adult life. Many times I heard my mother and others say, "They broke the mold when they made your father."

While I have not achieved the scale of living or the successes he enjoyed, I learned from him the values of honesty and courage, of fearlessness and gratitude, of giving without expectation of reward, and of friendship and fidelity. He always shared his wealth and good fortune with those around him and he prodded others who had more than him to give more than he did. He helped his employees and his friends attain things they never could have on their own, and he gave generously, anonymously, of his time and his money to education and research. As good a life as he had, he always believed the world could be a better place.

The Chief died at 64 of cancer a few days after the New Year in 1988. The months preceding his death were hard for him and for the many people who had come to depend on his generosity, guidance, and direction. Before his death, I spent weeks sleeping on a sofa in the outer room of the hospital suite where he lived out his last days, breaking only to fly to San Francisco for the New Years Grateful Dead shows, after he'd gone downhill following a final operation to relieve excruciating pain in his spine.

One of my sisters was apoplectic at my selfishness in abandoning him at the end in his virtual coma. "What if he *dies*," she screamed as I left for the airport. Two nights later, as I sat in my seat on the Jerry-side risers at the Oakland Coliseum, surrounded by five of my best friends, I felt the band play an epic rendition of *He's Gone* just for me, and I knew The Chief and I would be OK.

I returned home and though he never recognized my face or called me by my name again, I was able to hold him in my arms as he drew his last breath, to whisper in his ear, "I love you Dad, I love you so."

Six months later, a friend of mine, an A&R guy at Warner Bros. Records, who I had introduced to Muhammed Ali (a close pal of a friend of The Chief), thanked me for the introduction by taking me to Atlantic City for Ali's birthday party, where I sat next to Cheryl Tiegs at dinner and enjoyed the pleasure of shoving Donald Trump in the chest to make him sign my souvenir boxing glove.

The next night, we had ringside seats for the heavyweight championship fight between Mike Tyson and Larry Holmes. Before we got ready to leave for the arena, I went downstairs to the spa in the Trump Palace Hotel for a steam and a sauna, one of The Chief's most beloved guy rituals.

The place was empty as a tomb. I enjoyed the quiet and the stillness, and I thought about how much my dad would have loved doing what I was doing right then. I sat alone in the sauna when the cedar door creaked open, and in, through a shaft of bright yellow light, came a white-haired old man who moved slowly but who was clearly still in great shape for his age.

As my eyes adjusted again to the muted light of the sauna, I recognized the Yankee Clipper.

"I will be a motherfucker," I thought to myself.

"I'm sitting in the fucking sauna with Joe *fucking* DiMaggio!"

I'd heard legendary stories of DiMaggio's guarded nature and of his lust for privacy. I'd heard he could be a real prick. But I turned to him anyway and said, "Mr. DiMaggio, you don't know me, but I understand you were friends with my father back in New York and Miami in the forties and fifties. Buddy Lazar, from Avenue K in Brooklyn."

He looked at me, thinking.

"Yeah, I remember your father, how's he doing?"

I couldn't tell if he really remembered or if he was just being, what, friendly? Agreeable? "Well, you know, he always spoke very highly of you and he said you had some good times together, playing cards and running around some," I told him, which was exactly what my father had told me.

"I wouldn't bother you in this situation," I continued, "but I thought you'd want to know he passed away in January."

"I'm sorry," Joe DiMaggio told me. "Your father was a good guy."

I was happy to hear him say it, but I already knew that much. What I didn't know was that would probably be the closest I would ever come again to being in The Chief's footsteps.

MY MOTHER'S TALE – PART 1

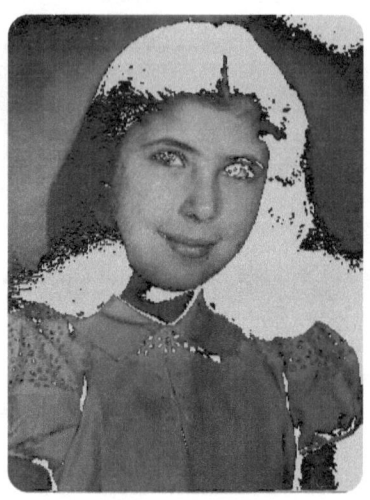

My mother was a smart, beautiful, Jewish gal from Brooklyn. She met my father in 1958 in Miami, when he had his personal assistant—in those days called a house man—deliver a note to the stunning little brunette who lived across the street and drove the red MG-TD, saying he'd like her to join him for dinner.

She was eleven years his junior but every bit his equal in almost every other way, and they quickly fell in love. They were married in my grandfather's Brooklyn living room the next year, and in 1960—the year I was born—they moved from Miami to Memphis, Tennessee, two East Coast Jews who knew almost nothing about the culture of the Dixie South, aside from the fact that everyone worth knowing had at least one maid and a yard man.

My parents were not rich, yet, but in the South at that time, even decidedly middle-class whites employed Black help. Elsewhere, I was born in the summertime, in Monticello, NY, in the Catskills, where my mother's family wrote insurance on the harness-racing horses and other livestock prevalent in the area. My mother's cousin had adopted two children in recent years and when I was born, the Sullivan County hospital doctor who delivered me called Joan and told her a healthy Jewish boy was available, and was she interested?

Joan's brood was sufficient, but she knew my mother was looking to adopt and she put in the call to Memphis. Within a week, arrangements had been made. My parents flew to New York to pick me up. I slept in a wicker laundry basket on the plane ride back to Memphis, and from every story I heard over the years, my parents were very happy. Years later, I saw some Super 8 footage of a trip they'd taken back to Miami in '62 or '63, clips of them both holding me and showing me off in front of the cabana at the pool of the apartment they kept there until around 1972. They looked very happy.

My father was a businessman, my mother a homemaker. She was quite involved with the Temple Sisterhood and for a while, when I was younger, she was a troop leader for the Girl Scouts, or maybe it was Brownies, I'm not sure. She was elegant and sophisticated, and seemed forever trying to raise the level of culture and discourse around her. She was an avid reader and had a wonderful sense of style: She wore beautiful clothes and decorated our home in a way I can only describe as hip.

Jackie Kennedy was destined for the White House when I came along and though I never confirmed it specifically with my mother, I believe she took inspiration in her sense of personal style from the elegant First Lady—they were similarly petite and brunette, though my mother had a fuller figure and a more ethnic look, which would serve her well later, in the 70s, when she adopted an Afro hairstyle and wore brightly-colored jumpsuits and tribal-patterned dresses.

15

Two things my mother loved above all were cooking and gardening. As a child, I spent hours in the kitchen with her and Minnie, our housekeeper. My mother never referred to Minnie as our maid, and when I did so once, when I was about 8, saying in a fit of pique and defiance, "I don't have to listen to you, you're just the maid…" my mother read me the riot act—and gave me my first glimpse into the ineffable mysteries of the human heart and the nature of compassion. In many ways, Minnie was my mother's best friend and together they cooked up wondrous things in the kitchen, cuisine that melded my mother's Jewish heritage (briskets and *kugels* and potato *knishes*), her love for all things Italian (linguini with white clam sauce, lasagne, chicken cacciatore) and Minnie's Alabama roots (fried chicken, BBQ pork, all kinds of greens, and the best lemon meringue pie, ever).

Tommy was our first yard man, who was always referred to as Minnie's husband, but I think that's because he sometimes slept with her in her apartment over our carport. He was jealous of Minnie's life with our family and was not always nice to her, but he worked hard with my mother in our yard, which backed up to a couple hundred acres of cornfield that was eventually turned into a subdivision sometime around '69 or '70.

My father ran Tommy off one day when I was about 7 or 8 after he left Minnie with an eye swollen shut from a fight they had. Soon we had Earl, who was "promoted" from his job as a warehouseman and truck driver at my father's business. Earl became our new yard man, my father's masseur and personal driver, the guy who drove school carpools (and years later taught me to drive a car), someone who worked for and was considered almost a member of our family for nearly twenty years. He would one day lead my father's funeral procession, driving The Chief's big white Mercedes-Benz at the head of a line of some 300 cars.

Before all that though, Earl worked like a mule with my mother, first in the yard on Chickasaw, then later when we moved into the old Crump place on Galloway, with its two-and-a-half acres of rolling landscaped yard, studded by towering, hundred year-old oak trees in the middle of Memphis. My mother was a fanatic for keeping the leaves raked, and the driveways swept, and she had dozens of flower beds to be kept weeded. She loved spending time in her custom-built greenhouse the size of a New York efficiency apartment, which she filled with exotic plants and flowers that couldn't stand the brutal Memphis summer heat or its bitter winter cold.

She and Earl had a tempestuous relationship due to his feeling he was more my father's man, having come from the business and all—and my father kept him busy enough with duties around the pool, with giving him a rubdown after his morning swim, or with driving him to this or that appointment—but to my mother, Earl was responsible for all the heavy lifting she needed in a man around the house, and she was never shy about having a list of chores for him to work at each day. Much to his dismay, she was willing to work as hard as any man with a rake or a broom or a hedge trimmer, and he sometimes struggled to keep up with her.

Years later, when I was old enough to be useful, my mother would press me into duty as well, having me rake leaves at the farthest edges of the property, or sweep dirt out at the ends of the circular drive. I would complain, "No one is ever going to see this. No one ever comes out here."

She'd look at me with a mixture of pity and disdain and say, "I know what's out here. I know what it looks like, and I want it clean and clear, got it?"

Mother's Day was a special day in our household, in part because my mother had a force of personality that demanded recognition on the day set aside for all mothers, but also because of my father's great love for her, and the sense we all had (I was the oldest of four, with a brother– also adopted–two years behind me, and two younger sisters my parents conceived together) of how much she gave to creating and nurturing her loving family and a loving home throughout the year.

When I was little, I gave her my own handmade Mother's Day cards, which she always thought were the most beautiful works of art she'd ever seen. A bit older, I'd go with my father to the florist to help him devise an arrangement of suitable grandeur or pick out something special for the yard or the greenhouse.

In my adolescence and early teen years, my facility with kitchen protocols began to emerge and she would thrill to the breakfasts of fresh fruit, omelets, pancakes or homemade waffles I would bring her in bed, with fresh juice and coffee (black, with one packet of Sweet n' Low).

I think I remember most, though, the last Mother's Day gift I gave her.

The summer I turned 17, I spent six weeks in the South of France with a family whose father was a business associate of my father's. They had two boys, 18 and 16 years old. We boys became fast friends and I learned a lot that summer, the least of which was twenty or thirty words of French. I hadn't wanted to leave at all, but when I returned home through New York, I was stunned to see my father there to greet me at the airport.

I had been expecting my grandfather to pick me up and planned to spend a couple of days with him before going home to Memphis. My father took little time cutting to the chase: while I was away, my mother had been diagnosed with lung cancer. She was recovering from surgery performed just days prior at Sloan-Kettering Memorial Hospital. One of her doctors was the same oncologist who had treated Brian Piccolo, the Chicago Bears running back who had died of lung cancer some years before, who made James Caan famous for playing him in the movie, "Brian's Song."

Treatment and understanding of lung cancer had progressed a lot since then, however, and we had reason to hope my mother's condition might be treatable. She came home before the start of school that fall and that winter we took a family trip, in January, to Monticello, NY. It was my first time back there since my birth. I got to meet my mother's cousin Joan and her adopted children, who were just a couple of years older than me.

Bruce Springsteen had recently released Born to Run and I learned Monticello was definitely Bruce country. I remember asking my cousins if they knew my favorite bands, Lynyrd Skynyrd and Tom Petty; they looked at me like I was from another planet. But we had great fun getting high and riding snowmobiles on their frozen lake at night, and I had no idea how much pain my mother was beginning to feel again.

By the spring, her cancer was back in full bloom and she began a new series of chemotherapy and radiation treatments that caused her to lose all her hair and made her very weak. She seemed to grow even smaller than her 5'2" frame would allow.

By the end of April, she was home and largely bedridden, and we all, except my youngest sister, who was not yet 8, understood she would soon die. On Mother's Day I crept into her room, dark and cool from curtains drawn against the bright sun and the approaching summer heat, to find her propped on pillows, sitting regally as ever, but with eyes closed.

I wasn't sure she could tell I was there. After a few moments, she opened her eyes and gave me a wan smile. I wished her a Happy Mother's Day and asked if I could do anything for her. She said, "You know what I'd like? I'd like a nice glass of fresh, cold orange juice. And open those curtains, I want to feel the sun."

I brightened the room for her and went to the kitchen to make up the juice. When I returned, her eyes were closed again, but she still had the little smile, and she took the juice from me with trembling hands. She held it a moment, then raised the glass to her lips and took several tiny sips before asking me to set it beside her on the nightstand.

I asked her if I could do anything else for her and she said, "No, I think I just want to rest now for a little bit."

I got home from school one day the next week and she was not in her room. My father was there and he told me they had come to take her to the hospital because she was in a lot of pain.

MY MOTHER'S TALE - PART 2

My mother came to America from Lithuania in the early 1950s as a young girl. Her younger sister, parents, and her maternal grandparents made up the family that settled in Brooklyn, NY. Her father, a well-known playwright and artist whose paintings hang today in the national gallery at Vilnius, was an ardent anti-communist who had flown, reluctantly I am told, fighter planes for the Luftwaffe in the Second World War. He placed his girls in a convent not far from Brooklyn, but my mother kept running away, unable to bear the nuns' cruelty.

By the time she was 13 or 14, her father relented and allowed the girls to live in an apartment they all shared above a candy shop in the Williamsburg area. One night in the fall of 1959, my mother accompanied a friend of her father's to a nightclub, where they saw a performer whose act was not unlike others of the period—song and dance comedy in the mold of Martin & Lewis or Joey Bishop.

My mother was starstruck and told her chaperone she wanted to meet the young entertainer. After the show, he came out from backstage to greet the pair, where he took one look at my mother, stuck out his hand, and said, "OK, I'll marry you!"

The two of them would indeed marry several years later, well after the finest parts of their relationship had been taken away, or destroyed, by neglect and abuse and ignorance. But in that moment, they were both consumed by infatuation, by passion and desire that would take them on a journey across thousands of miles and nearly a lifetime of experience crammed into a tiny window of time.

My grandfather was not happy with his friend for introducing his daughter to such a man. He forbade my mother from seeing the young entertainer. But the singer persisted and took to serenading her from the street outside the candy shop, which eventually softened my grandmother's heart toward him, and the two lovebirds began to secretly rendezvous with her blessing on the fire escape at the back of my mother's apartment building.

Soon he was meeting her after school and the two of them explored all the things young lovers do in the parks and museums and other public spaces of New York. It should come as no surprise that my mother turned up pregnant in the spring of 1960, or that this caused no end of shame and bad feelings for everyone involved. Fortunately, by the end of the school year, she was only just beginning to show her baby bump, and it was decided the best thing for everyone might be if she accompanied my father to the Catskill Mountains upstate, where he was booked for a summer-long series of engagements in the showrooms of the area's Borscht Belt resorts. There she could stay out of trouble and have her baby away from the prying, judgmental eyes of her neighbors.

Danny Dawson was a twenty-five year-old libertine, an alcoholic hustler with a quick, pornographic wit and a golden voice, the youngest of fourteen kids from a working-class Irish family from Philly. A former altar boy who was ever anything but, and who was also anything but prepared to settle down and raise a family.

My mother was sheltered, a still-mostly-innocent school-girl, with a pretty face and a great rack, who'd fallen hard for the charming entertainer and would follow him to the ends of the earth at that point. But she wasn't prepared to raise a family either, and though she told me later she'd have been willing to be a single mom, she was completely oblivious to the plan her mother and Dawson had devised to put me up for adoption.

The day I was born, my mother had a hard time pushing me through her birth canal and as was typical of OB/GYN practice then, she was sedated so a surgeon could cut her open and deliver me into this lifetime. When she awoke from the anesthesia, her mother, Dawson, and the doctors told my mother I had died in childbirth and that they were all so, so, very sorry.

Dawson told her the baby had been born with a hole in his heart. My mother was 16 years old.

Thirty-seven years later, telling me the story of my birth, she claimed she never believed I had died, despite the fact that no one, not Dawson, her parents, nor the hospital (to which she had returned again and again in succeeding years in a fruitless search for the truth of what had happened to her on August 8, 1960), none ever admitted they had given her child away.

For years afterward, she told me, after she had married and divorced Dawson, when she married her husband Tom and had my half-sister and a half-brother, she would sit sometimes with them, and tell them about me. She said they would look to the sky for the brightest star they could find and say a prayer for me, the child she was never sure she had.

Never sure, that is, until the day in 1997 when Dan Dawson called her out of the blue and she, having neither seen nor spoken to him since running into him by chance in a Fort Lauderdale bar twenty five years before, was there to take his call.

"I knew it was you," she responded, after Dawson handed me the phone and I'd said, "Hi, mom!" Though almost nothing could have surprised me in those first whirlwind weeks when I met my birth parents, I raised my eyebrows and said, "Oh really? How did you know?"

She told me she had always been a sensitive person, someone people thought of as superstitious, if not exactly clairvoyant, and that she had been thinking a lot about the baby she was never sure she had during the past several weeks. She'd been standing in a checkout line at the grocery store about a week before, when someone she did not know at all turned around and said to her, mysteriously, with no further explanation, "someone you have not seen in a very long time is trying to find you."

At first, when Dawson called, she'd thought it was him this person had been referring to, but when he said, "hold on, someone wants to say hello," before I could say, "Hi, mom," she said she knew it was me.

Within days I was on a plane to Pittsburgh to finally meet my mother, a person I had wondered about and dreamed of nearly my whole life, especially so since the mother I had grown up with, the woman I had always called and thought of as mom, who had loved me so very well and taught me so much, who had given me my appreciation for art and music and food and style, and for so many of the things I value most in life and about people, had died when I was 17.

That first night, after I'd gotten to meet her husband and my new half-siblings, after everyone but my mother and I had gone to bed, the two of us stayed up late, talking. She told me the story of my birth and I told her the story of my childhood, and we looked into each other's eyes and knew an indescribable kind of love, the kind of love that can only be known by total strangers who had spent a lifetime thinking about one another, without ever knowing for sure the other existed.

After the deluge of words, when there was nothing left, at that moment, to say, I laid my head in her lap, curled into a ball, and she stroked my just-beginning-to-grey hair while I cried like a baby.

WHO ARE YOU?

I was born Daniel Joseph Dawson, Jr., to parents listed on my birth certificate as Daniel and Loreta Dawson. I had rarely considered tracking either of them down before my adoptive parents were gone, but in my 30s the idea began to take root. I first began searching not long after I discovered that birth certificate and my adoption papers in my father's files after his death in 1988 and turned initially to the telephone book for Sullivan County in New York, where I'd been born.

I couldn't have known Daniel and Loreta were long gone from New York by the late 80s, that they had made their way after my birth down to south Florida, like so many other north-easterners who populated the big rush to Florida's "Gold Coast" during the 50s and 60s. Facing the first of what would prove to be many dead ends I'd encounter during the next nine years, I set my search aside and turned to moving myself and my new wife out to California, where I knew my destiny lay.

Once we got settled in San Francisco, we busied ourselves with the joys of living in paradise, taking time to explore the Golden State and partake of its dusky charms. In the fall of 1992 I received a package from my wife's sister, who was working at the time in a Memphis law firm. She had run a search to find every Daniel and Loreta Dawson in the LEXIS database. Her file contained over a hundred Daniel, Daniel Js, and Daniel Josephs, and almost two dozen Loretas and Lorettas. A form letter was written. Bulk mailings commenced. A few letters came back undeliverable, the rest drew no response. In time, the search gave way to the rhythms of daily life, where I helped run a funky little nightclub in the Haight/Fillmore, writing songs and learning to play the guitar in my spare time, while my wife worked at the airport as a customer service agent.

We thought about having a child ourselves but found frustration and sadness along the way in two miscarriages between the end of 1995 and the fall of 1996, which probably increased my desire to learn more about my genetic background. So I turned again to searching for Dawsons throughout the country, focusing my attention on using tools I found on the rapidly expanding Internet. Interestingly enough, in thinking of this search, I had always visualized, thought of, considered, and yearned for my mother. In my mind, my father was a shadowy figure, a man of mystery who had never figured prominently in the very sketchy pictures I'd been given about those lazy summer days at the dawn of the Sixties: my mother had been a dancer, perhaps, or was somehow connected to the entertainment people who plied the Borscht Belt crowds; she was Jewish. They thought she had been quite young.

In the spring of 1997, I decided I would return to Monticello, to pore over whatever records the New York Department of Public Health, or the hospital, or the courts would make available to me. By this time, I had registered with a few adoption registries I'd found on the Internet, hoping perhaps my birth parents had come to know of them and register, too. It seemed the tide of information was beginning to turn in favor of putting adoptees and their birth parents in touch with one another, though New York's rules for the exchange of information remained among the nation's most conservative. I contacted relatives in Monticello, and forewarned them of my intentions. I soon got a call from Joan, who'd played go-between in my adoption, and through her connection to the local baby doc, put the prospective parents in contact with the hospital where the baby was born.

She welcomed me to visit New York now, some thirty-seven years later, and graciously offered accommodations for my stay. But she also gave me information I'd never received before: details about some of the players involved, which would prove crucial to completing my search. A prominent resort of the time, one of the few remaining in business today, was Kutscher's. Its matriarch, Helen Kutscher, was still alive and might remember if any entertainers named Dawson had played her showroom at the time I was born. The Rapp Agency booked many of the entertainers back then, out of New York City, whose current head was Howard Rapp; he might be a source of information to help my search.

What proved the key to a still unravelling mystery, though, was the artist's guild to which many entertainers in the Catskills had belonged, The American Guild of Variety Artists.

Michael sounded busy when he answered AGVA's telephone in their Manhattan office. He had the brusque manner typical of a harried New Yorker; he seemed almost offended to have had his day interrupted by the ringing of the telephone. I got right to the point. I was looking for a social security number or address for a couple of people who might have been AGVA members thirty or forty years ago. His first response was to say that he wouldn't have that information. But then, as if a light went on somewhere in Michael's brain, and he saw the route to a diversion from his workaday routine, he caught himself and asked, "why do you need this information?"

I laid it out. I said I'd been born in Monticello 37 years ago, and placed for adoption by parents I believed were entertainers in the area, whom I also believed might have been members of AGVA. My search for my birth parents had led me to make this call, and if there was any way to access old membership records, I would appreciate anything that might help narrow my search.

Michael said he'd take a look in the microfilm files stored in the basement when he had a chance, and would call back if he found anything. It must have been a slow day in the AGVA offices, because Michael called me back about two hours later with a social security number for one Daniel Dawson, together with a 1955 address in Philadelphia, and a 1959 address in Brooklyn, NY.

He'd found no records for a Loretta Dawson. I couldn't believe it. I was getting close. A social security number meant I had an actual, identifiable person. I went to the Social Security Death Index maintained by the Social Security Administration and checked to see if this particular Daniel Dawson had died. I was relieved to find no record of death for the SS# in question, but since the index only shows persons for whom a final lump sum death benefit has been paid, I didn't get too excited.

My next step was contacting an old friend of The Chief, one of a very few with whom I'd managed to stay in touch over the nearly ten years since my father's death. Ted had been the FBI's top man in the southeast region, who became friendly with my dad in the early 70s. I'd stayed close with him after he retired from government service to become a renowned private investigator, a best-selling author, and radio talk-show host. I figured, if I knew anyone who could find someone with a social security number, Ted would be the man.

Ted was happy to help me out. He averred it might take some time, as he was on a case at the moment, so it could be a few weeks before I'd hear from him. After such a long time searching (in my heart and mind, if not actively at work on the actual search), I figured I could wait another few weeks. But even at that, I didn't have to. Not two nights later, Ted's voice was on the answering machine at my nightclub: "Lonnie, Ted here. We got your Dad. I'm leaving town early tomorrow, so call me as soon as you can and I'll give you the information."

I was stunned. I'd found my father.

It was nearly eleven o'clock in the evening when I reached Ted. Yes, he was sure it was the right Daniel Dawson. The social security number and the addresses were a match; he had two telephone numbers and an address in Gulfport, Mississippi. I asked if he had any more information: was he married, did he have any kids? Ted chuckled and said, "Hey, Lonnie. I could build you a whole profile on the guy if you want. But that takes time and costs money. Here's his phone number, call him and ask him yourself."

THESE ARE MY PEOPLE

The Dawson clan came to the United States from County Kerry, Ireland, during The Great Potato Famine in the mid-19th century. They settled near Philadelphia and, along with other working-class Europeans who made up the second big wave of immigration to the "New World," began their pursuit of the American Dream.

By the late 1950s, Daniel Joseph Dawson had left his days as a Philadelphia altar boy behind, said goodbye to his parents and thirteen siblings, and become "The Dynamic Danny Dawson," trying his best to make it in showbiz. He worked clubs around New York in the late 50s as a singer, dancer, and comedian, often performing as the MC for variety shows popular at the time. Known as a "white Sammy Davis, Jr.," he was a gifted mimic with a sweet singing voice.

One night in the spring of 1959, he sat in his dressing room backstage at a Brooklyn nightclub when his manager burst in very excited. "Denny,

Denny! You got to come meet this goil, Denny! She's beautiful, like Hollywood, I'm telling you!" Danny had heard this before, and wasn't particularly in the mood after a long night on stage. He would have preferred to get out of his wet clothes and head home for a nice long soak in a hot bath. But his manager persisted. So Danny followed him out onto the floor, where he saw the back of a gorgeous, built-like-a-brickhouse blonde. As she turned for the introduction, the irrepressible comic stretched out his hand and said, "OK—I'll marry ya!"

They would, actually, one day marry. But that would come several years later, after many adventures and discoveries, and after the birth of their son, who would come along thirty seven years after the fact to spark a reunion with reverberations and repercussions that echo through the generations to this day.

Dan had married his fourth wife, Cathy, in the late 70s. She tossed my letter on the desk one afternoon in the first week of October '97, and said to Dan, "You're gonna LOVE this one." She watched as he read the letter, which basically said, "Hi, I'm your long-lost son, wondering if you can give me any information about my genetic background and heritage." He looked up from his glasses and said, "It's true." He had never told anyone about the child he'd fathered with Lore Dawson (his second wife), or about how they had given him up for adoption in the summer of 1960, when they were both too young and unprepared to start a family. He called his daughter, one of two he'd had by his third wife, Sylvia, whom he'd divorced in 1975. Danie lived just down the block, in the same apartment complex where Dan and Cathy lived, across the street from the fine white sands of Long Beach, Mississippi, on the shores of the Gulf of Mexico.

Danie came into his office, where he proceeded to tell her and Cathy the story of little Danny Dawson, Jr., and he composed an email to send in response to the letter he'd received that day.

I sat staring at my computer screen for several minutes, trying to digest the subject heading that appeared in my email in-box:

YES! YOU FOUND YOUR BIRTH FATHER!!

It had been almost a week since I'd sent my letter, and I sat now, trembling and breathing heavily as I contemplated reading the first words I'd ever had from my birth father. To this point I'd known nothing about him, and I still didn't know if my birth mother was dead or alive, or whether I would ever be able to find her.

It blew my mind to read that not only had my father been in show business back in the late 50s, he'd continued to write and record songs into the 70s. Now, at the age of 62, in the waning years of the century, he was fully in step with the tech revolution. He even had a website where he hawked his tunes!

I had awakened to my own long-dormant love for music near the end of my studies in law, and I'd spent the succeeding twelve years working a variety of "day jobs" to pay the bills while I struggled to find my voice, plumbed for the bottom of my groove, and hoped to one day make a living as a singer & songwriter. To learn now it had been in my genes all along was a synchronicity too wild to contemplate.

I reeled further to learn Dan had spent time recording in Memphis when I was in high school, and that he'd had offices in Metairie, outside New Orleans, during the time I had been learning the meaning of *lassiez les bon temps rouler* at Tulane. The near-tangents were too eerie to think possible.

From a flurry of emails that commenced between us immediately, and through several long telephone conversations in those first few days, I learned how Danny Dawson and Lorecka Juodis, a beautiful young immigrant from Lithuania, had come to meet and to fall in love. And because he thoroughly enjoyed the craft of storytelling, I learned how they married, and fell out of love, separated, and went their own ways more than thirty years ago.

Dan told me about my mother, about her family, a younger sister, and a beautiful, engaging mother who took pity on him even as her husband, my grandfather Juodis, banned his daughter from fraternizing with the young entertainer. Dan's recollections of his youth, of his life with the woman he called his "one really big love," were filled with romance and excitement, with tales of living by their wits in New York, of their friendships with other entertainers of the era, like Lenny Bruce, Rodney Dangerfield, and Jackie Mason.

I heard about how Danny & Lore, as they had been known together, moved from New York to Miami in the early 60s, where their relationship eventually foundered on the shoals of the sexual revolution and the era's infatuation with pharmaceutical libertarianism. Dan had last seen Lore sometime in the 70s, after they had been divorced nearly ten years; he'd had no contact with her since. He thought she had at least one child, and had remarried, but he really wasn't sure.

The similarities between my new father's life and what I knew of The Chief's seemed striking. Both men had come of age in Brooklyn. They had each made their way to South Florida, and travelled in, if not the same circles, at least knew some of the same people who were active in show business in the late 50s. Before founding his wine & liquor distributorship, The Chief had owned nightclubs in Miami, had spent a brief period booking the comedy team of Red Foxx & Slappy White, while Dan himself performed as an entertainer in and around New York in the same era. In the 60s, Dan was involved in a loan situation with the reputed mobster Jimmy Blue Eyes, who, it turns out, was a friend of The Chief and would be a guest at my Bar Mitzvah in 1973. They both were independent go-getters with decided gifts for gab. They could talk to anyone, from kings to street tramps, and they both found it preferable to work for themselves. They each had to be the boss; neither cottoned to working for one. The Chief sold air conditioners in Havana in the early 50s, while Dan sold cars in Daytona in the 60s.

As a young man, Danny Dawson had been brazen and outrageous enough to transform a working-class lapsed-Irish Catholic hustler into a quick talking MC and comic, complete with a dead-on Yiddish accent and *meshuggeneh* vocabulary to match, not a stunt just any goyim could pull off. He ran his Daytona car dealership for many years, working hard as the head of a family of six (along with his third wife Sylvia, her two kids from a previous marriage, and the two daughters they produced together) to put food on the table and see to it his kids grew up with strong values and tools for making their own ways in life.

The Chief had been as much a lapsed Jew as Dan was a lapsed Catholic. He used to say, about his place as a Jew in the South, "Well, you know, we're Reform Jews. In fact, we're so reformed, we're almost Episcopalian." But like Dan's attendance at Christmas Mass every year, The Chief went to synagogue on High Holy Days, and presided yearly in his inimitable way over the Passover Seder. He sent me to Sunday school, and laid on a memorable feast and celebration in honor of my "passage into manhood" at Thirteen.

Talking with Dan was like having a conversation with myself. I had been following the development of the Internet since about 1992, when a good friend turned from selling computers to laying the foundation for one of the first Internet Service Providers in the Bay Area. To find my birth father interested in computers and the Internet was a heartening sign.

But email could not contain or convey the amount, nor express the depth of the information and sentiment to which we had finally uncorked the bottle. After a week of long telephone conversations and a dozen email exchanges, I broached the topic of meeting Dan face to face. He was not only receptive to the idea, he encouraged me to come visit, to meet the family, and stay down in Gulfport as long as I wanted. In the meantime, he had gone to work trying to track down my mother.

Just before I was to leave San Francisco, I learned Dan had located Lore's social security number through a place she'd worked as a cocktail waitress some twenty five years before. I got back on the phone to Ted with the news in no time, and a request for him to work his magic once again. Ted was happy to oblige, though he had to charge his usual fee for this one.

My plane landed at the small airport in Gulfport at 9:38 in the evening. It was already well dark and seemed later than it was because there was hardly anyone around. I recognized Dan and he me from the pictures we'd already exchanged through email, but my first thought when I saw him was, "Am I gonna look like *that* in a few years?"

Dan was fit enough for a man his age, with a bit of a paunch, a full head of gray-speckled hair and a matching beard set off by a winning smile that was diminished only by the absence of several teeth back along the jawline. I asked about the teeth and he shrugged and said he'd still have them if he'd taken better care of himself.

We drove a short distance to one of the casinos in nearby Biloxi and took a booth in the cafe off the main gaming floor. Though neither of us were strangers to the casino environment, we weren't there for action. We just wanted a comfortable place to talk some things out, and the casino never closed.

Talk we did, too, till well past midnight, sharing stories about our amazingly coincident experiences in life. He told me the story (from his perspective, of course) of meeting my mother, of wooing her, and of the difficulties with her parents and how he overcame them. He told me how he eventually won over my grandmother's heart and how, even after he'd begun sleeping with my 16-year-old mother, he ended up sleeping with her mother, too.

He related an incredible tale of the night my grandfather finally let down his defenses against the guy in love with his daughter, how he played cards and drank vodka with all of them till the wee hours, and after my mother had gone to sleep, how he ended up fucking both of her parents in drunken debauchery.

He sat across the formica-topped table between us in the booth, staring holes in me, and marveled, "You look just like your mother."

He told me about the scheme he'd hatched with my grandmother to put me up for adoption, unbeknownst to my mother, and how he earned a $5,000 bonus for telling the adoption agency my mother was Jewish. He admitted they had all lied to my mother, telling her I had died in childbirth, though he didn't relate the detail about my having been born with a hole in my heart—that I learned a week later, when I heard my mother's version of the story.

After he'd talked himself out I was spinning, dizzied by all of this new information about where I'd come from and about the lives of the people who'd brought me into this world. Dan had booked me a hotel room at a place between the casino and his apartment on the beach, but said they had a guest room I was welcome to stay in. That first night, I thanked him for the hotel room, relieved to have a place where I could repair alone, to consider everything I'd just heard, and to ponder the meanings and the possibilities.

I undressed and climbed into bed in the darkened room, and began to shiver and shake uncontrollably, which had nothing to do with the temperature inside the room or outside on the Gulf of Mexico. I realized I had, for the first time in my life, embraced and been embraced by a blood relative. The effects of that realization shot through me as massive currents of energy through a newly opened portal, stretching far into the past and defining, now and forevermore, something inescapable about the future.

I curled into a fetal posture, hugging my knees to my chest as my teeth chattered and my eyes seemed to spin backward into the top of my skull. I don't know how long it took me to finally fall asleep but I know I didn't move or stop shaking until I did."

OCTOBER 6, 1999—SAN FRANCISCO

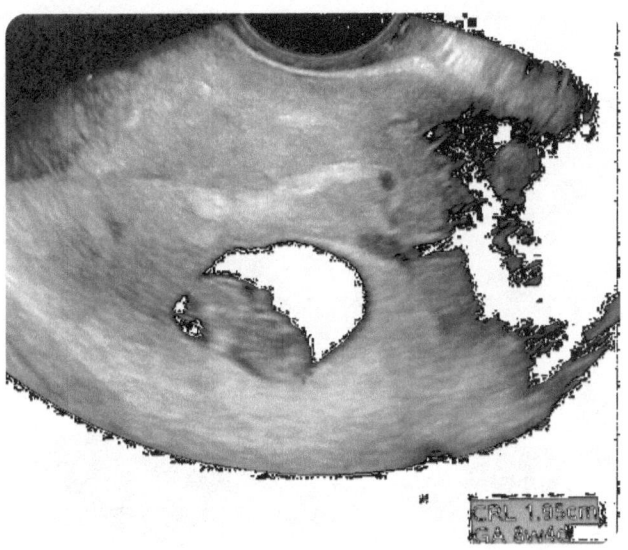

It's been a few weeks more now and we've been keeping a pretty close eye and ear on you. We've seen the birth staff three times since the day we first saw you via ultrasound. Your mom has had some blood tests, we've checked you out by ultrasound a couple of times—today we heard your heartbeat for the first time. It was quite moving: our midwife, Judith, first found your mom's heartbeat, which was a steady sixty-five beats per minute. Then, after some deft manipulation of the ultrasonic listening device, she picked up yours. An astounding 135 beats per minute! You were jamming! We were both so excited. Your mom's eyes sparkled so brightly as she looked from the little device on her belly going...

boomboomboomboomboomboomboomboomboom

ALL DOWN THE LINE: A FAVOR FOR KEITH RICHARDS

Dude, I really need your help." My buddy's voice is insistent, though not frantic. I know the difference with him. He is a successful salesman at a big firm and we go back a long way. As kids, we used to get in fights on the football field or the basketball court, before he got big enough to earn the nickname "Bear," which comes from his size as well as the amount of hair he ended up with all over his body, but also because deep down, he is as gentle and true as just about any friend you'd ever want to have.

We are in our early thirties now, and when Bear gets insistent with you, you buy the thing he's talking about. He didn't get to be successful insisting people make shitty purchases, although lots of folks wonder about a stock broker who calls himself Bear. The last time I'd heard him sound *frantic* was when he'd called from the county jail after they'd busted him trying to pick up 500 hits of Ecstasy at the airport.

FedEx had called and said, "Mr. B, we have your package but we were unable to deliver it this morning; could you come by and pick it up, please?"

Oops.

Bear knew it was important to keep that little episode out of the papers and as far from his employers' notice as possible. Since I had a little personal experience with a similar predicament, I was his one phone call from the pokey. I was honored, actually, and it ended up working out pretty satisfactorily. But now, today, when I hear that insistent tone, it's a different story, and since I don't have any investments with him, I'm curious.

"What's happenin', bro?"

"I need you to fly here and drive to New Orleans with me next weekend."

Now, I certainly don't need any particular excuse to go to New Orleans, it being one of my all-time favorite cities and the place where I formed many lifelong predilections, habits, and ideas concerning the proper balance between work and play. But I'm in San Francisco now, and the thought of flying a couple thousand miles, only to climb into a car and drive four or five hours through the Mississippi Delta to New Orleans, is not exactly my idea of a super-fun excursion, even if Bear does drive a BMW750 Turbo.

"Dude, you're not gonna believe this, but I have to drive Keith fucking Richards' guns to New Orleans, and I don't want to do it alone. If you come, we'll have backstage passes to the show and maybe even get a chance to hang out with Keith. No promises, but man, c'mon. You're the only one I'm willing to do this with."

"Bear, don't fuck with me."

"I'm serious, man. Please."

"How did you end up with Keith Richards' guns?"

"My buddy is Keith's personal assistant. He's coming in from Nashville before they play there on Wednesday. He says Keith is spooked about the cops in the South and he doesn't want to chance taking anything funky on the charter. Our dude says he will totally take care of us in New Orleans."

I think about all that for a moment and say, "Well, fuckin'-A, Bubba. Count me in."

Like I said, no particular excuse.

Bear picks me up at the airport on Friday night and we plan to hit the road first thing in the morning, to arrive in New Orleans before lunch. So we take it easy. After a few drinks at the Lobby Bar in the Peabody Hotel, we catch the second set of the Willys on Beale Street, then make the last set of deep blues at Greens Lounge out off Airways Blvd.

Greens is a low-slung, cinder block roadhouse on the wrong side of the tracks in the weird, light-industrial/semi-residential flats out near the airport, where the city only managed to buy out a portion of the old-time sharecroppers' places that had been out that way for a hundred years or so before they put the airport there in the 60s. It's the kind of place where you get frisked going in the door, where they have signs stencilled on the walls: *NO GUNS OR KNIVES ALLOWED; NO CUSSING; NO DOPE SMOKING*. If you ask the bartender for a beer, she'll say, "You want a can or a quart, Sugar?" They play real blues at Greens.

We're semi-sober and tucked in at Bear's house before 3:00 a.m., no problem.

We decide to take 61 South through Clarksdale and Vicksburg to Baton Rouge before picking up 10 East into New Orleans instead of making the straight shot down I-55 through Jackson, even though 55 would be a faster trip. The long way is a prettier ride, hugging the pine bluffs closer to the river, where miles and miles and endless miles of cotton fields and soybeans and sorghum and corn are far less blemished by billboards and towering fast food beacons than is the federal highway. Plus, we figure the smaller roads will be an incentive not to wind up Bear's Beemer and risk unwanted attention from the Mississippi Highway Patrol.

It could have worked out differently, but we end up rolling into the Big Easy about 3:00 in the afternoon with Keith's 9-mm Barretta and his awesome blue steel Smith & Wesson model 29–6 .44 magnum with a freaking 8½-inch barrel wrapped safe and sound in Bear's duffel bag in the back seat. The Stones and crew are staying at the Ritz-Carlton down on Canal Street, not ten minutes from the Superdome, and when we call, Bear's friend says they're just getting back to the hotel from the afternoon soundcheck. We go up to the room, where Bear gladly unburdens himself of the duffle bag, tossing it on one of the double beds.

Our dude hands over two tickets to the show. Our seats are on the floor, about twenty rows back from the stage, and who am I to complain about free tickets to a Stones show? Bear hems and haws and we can both tell his friend is under a tremendous amount of stress. A small, dark-featured guy with thin lips, close-set eyes, and a three-day stubble, he has the fast cadences and clipped, abrupt manner that betray his

New York roots. He's visibly uncomfortable, sweating freely in New Orleans' subtropical humidity, as he fields half a dozen calls to both his cell phone and the room phone in the ten minutes we sit with him.

Everyone is relieved when Bernard Fowler, one of the Stones' trio of excellent back-up singers, pokes his head in the room and immediately recognizes Bear from his days as a doorman at the Hard Rock Cafe in New York. They share a warm hug and Bear introduces me. Bernard is relaxed and friendly and invites us both to come hang out in his room so Keith's PA can do his thing. As we leave, our dude calls out, "Bear, just call my cell when you get to the venue. I'll get you guys hooked up."

We stroll down the hall and enter a room where colorful tapestries hang over the heavy, flocked curtains covering the windows. Gauzy fabrics flung haphazardly over every light fixture lend a kind of opium den atmosphere to the place, an effect enhanced by the burning incense and vaguely middle-eastern trance-dance music lilting from a portable stereo system perched on the dresser. Bear and Bernard are rapping about New York and the current tour, and Bernard speaks as if in a dream about how much fun he's having working for Mick Jagger, who was and is and always has been the boss, at least when the band is on the road.

Bernard pulls out a huge fatty that we pass around as I listen to the two chums catch up, while I sink deeper and deeper into a plush easy chair and try to take in my surroundings, thinking, "Well, it's not hanging out with Keith, but it's still pretty cool."

Lisa Fischer, Bernard's stunning singing mate, comes in and stays for a while. My gaze lingers on her beautiful, smooth brown skin and her big, bright smile, and I appreciate how full of life and happiness she seems. She and Bernard are both easygoing and hospitable, happy to share whatever good fortune they have with us, which, such as it is, can't extend much beyond their friendly good humor and the contents of Bernard's mini-bar—but both are open and offered, and we gladly partake.

After about an hour, Lisa excuses herself to go get ready for the show and Bernard says he has to start getting it together, too, so Bear and I get up to take our leave. We haven't eaten since a quick breakfast before hitting the road, followed by perfect greasy cheeseburgers in Vicksburg, and between Bernard's kick-ass weed and the several beers we've each had in the room, we're both light on our feet.

We're spending the night at my friend Mad Dog's, uptown, but by now it's already past 5:00 p.m. If we go up there before the show we won't make it back to the Dome before the Stones are ready to go on at about 9:15, so we do what any couple of self-respecting traveling dudes would do and head down to the Ritz bar, where we order a round of Sazeracs and take turns going to the restroom off the lobby to freshen up.

Fortunately, the bar has free appetizers. We put a little ballast in the tanks, surveying the scene like lords and gentlemen, knowing we have an In to the event everyone in town is either going to, or wants to go to on this special Saturday. Even New Orleans, with its *lassiez les bon temps rouler* mantra and its parade of Festivals, its meetings and conventions, and Super Bowls, championship fights, and every big goddamned party anyone ever wanted to throw down in North America—even The City That Care Forgot—gets a little sideways when the Stones are in town.

Energy in the bar and the lobby is starting to ramp, with rockers young and old, tattered and elegant, hip-shaking and sashaying up and down the carpeted halls, hoping to see somebody or be seen by somebody, to-a-one (I tell myself), living an attitude that says, "If you can't rock me, somebody will."

We finish our drinks and hit the street for the walk across Canal and up Poydras to the Superdome. Soon, nearly 40,000 people will revel here in an electrocharged space the Rolling Stones have commanded for a quarter-century, taking it many times all over the globe. In it, the band have amassed unfathomable personal wealth, by an unmatched combination of bravado and artistry, showmanship and theater, where they have literally written the script for *The Story of Rock and Roll*.

We're borne along on waves of people shouting, laughing, waving go-cups large and small, and I'm struck by the diversity around me. Almost everyone is white, to be sure, but three and four generations are here. People older than the Stones themselves, who are at or pushing fifty; people ten and fifteen years older than me. Swarms of beautiful, stupid kids in their teens and twenties, wearing tight clothes or not much clothes at all, tempting us and each other with what my doctor friends call *young tissue*. And kids, real kids, eight and ten and twelve and younger, two and five, in their mothers' arms, all streaming through the night—and I think, "*Exile on Main Street*; got it."

IN THE VOODOO LOUNGE

We get up to the gate and Bear is pounding the keys of his cellphone. In a minute he's going, "Ok. Ok. Right. See you in a few." We go in at field level and look for a stairway off the outer concourse. We follow bare cinder block walls to a part of the building resembling hallways and kitchens in hotels and convention centers I've had occasion to haunt, with awful fluorescent lighting buzzing overhead, grating, clanging noises echoing off the concrete walls, and finally, down a narrow passageway at the end of which sits one of the largest, roundest black men I have ever seen, wearing a white polo shirt.

The door he's sitting in front of calls to mind the rabbit hole in *Alice's Adventures in Wonderland*, and I think, "here come the 'shrooms." Bear's friend, Keith's assistant who kindled our adventure, appears behind the security dude, looking far more pleased with the world than when we left him at the Ritz.

Bear and I squeeze through the rabbit hole into a vast warren of circus-tented rooms and hallways. It takes a few to get the lay of the land, but it's soon clear there's a large reception area with tables and chairs and several troughs of beverages, where maybe a hundred people are milling around buffet tables stacked with crudite and light snacks, behind which another little hallway runs, on either side of which is a game room and another reception area, this one with plush couches, loveseats and easy chairs, where TV monitors show the opening acts absolutely no one in here is interested in onstage out in the arena.

There are buckets of cold beer, red wine and white, and sumptuous trays of hot foods: jambalaya, red beans and rice, soft-shelled crab po' boys and oysters and crawfish, prime rib, and salads, and sweets. In no time, our dude is gone and there we are, me and Bear, backstage at the Rolling Stones show in the Louisiana Superdome.

We nibble on some crabs and go check out the game room. In the center is a huge snooker table, where Ronnie Wood is proceeding to show a bemused looking fellow in his forties the meaning of putting "English" on the ball. There are maybe a dozen, fifteen people in here, among whom is [MC] Hammer, over in the corner, furiously jukking an old-school pinball machine. I'm thinking, "Bro, you are gonna *tilt*!"

Suddenly Mick Jagger flits in from an inner sanctum that surprisingly has no physical barrier before it, but which no one seems to venture toward. Still no sign of Keith, but with Mick's elfin appearance the energy in the room lifts, and suddenly someone is introducing him to Hammer, who whips out a cassette tape and an imploring look. Mick seems put off, but graciously guides *Hammer Time* over toward a stereo system, where the tape is popped into a deck and I hear a rudimentary track of beats and rhythms while Hammer starts to do a live rap.

He's wearing a matching top and pants that look like nothing so much as oversized pajamas, money-green on black, with gold trim, and he's a dancin' fool. Mick never looks him in the eye, from what I can see, but he stands there, with his head cocked a little bit like he's actually listening, bobbing his shiny, fluffy locks in time to the beat, with his arms crossed, tapping a toe, for about thirty seconds. I hear him say, "It's great to meet you, man." He grabs both of MC Hammer's hands and then darts back to the inner rooms. Hammer Time is over.

By now, Ronnie's snooker game is done, too. Hammer gets back on the pinball machine in the corner, and I spot Charlie Watts, wearing a grey turtleneck and navy blazer, standing by the snooker rail talking to no one, looking for all the world like a middle school principal standing in the rec room at some Anglican seminary.

I'd told a few friends about making this trip and two of them, unbeknownst to each other, living on opposite coasts of the country, each said to me: "if you get to meet Charlie Watts, kiss him for me." How could I not? I stride confidently up to the much-beloved drummer of the Greatest Rock and Roll Band in the World, stick out my hand and say, "Hi Charlie, my name is Lonnie Lazar and I'm here from San Francisco; thanks so much for your hospitality."

Charlie's hand is soft, his skin smooth, with nails well manicured and polished, but his grip is firm, and he says to me in a quiet voice, "I love San Francisco, it's a beautiful place."

"You know, a guy like me doesn't often find himself backstage at a Rolling Stones concert," I say unnecessarily, adding, "I told all my friends, of course, that I was gonna be here, and two of them said to me, 'You gotta kiss Charlie Watts for me if you get to meet him.'"

I'm still a very respectful distance away from Charlie at this point, though I am certain he doesn't mistake me for a stone-cold-sober guy, or even a completely harmless fellow. I see a tiny wave of horror cross his face as he contemplates whether I am about to embrace him on behalf of my unnamed friends.

"But I'm not gonna do that, OK?" I say. And he adds, right as the words are out of my mouth, "Thanks very much, really."

We chat for another couple of minutes about New Orleans and the tour, and I ask him about his dogs because I've read that he and his wife have a whole bunch of them, big ones, and that they sleep in the bed with them, and he says, "Yes, they do," and tells me that he really loves them and misses them when he's out on tour and he thanks me for coming, and hopes I enjoy the show.

Bear comes back around and we drift into the room with the hot food, which is starting to empty out because the band will take the stage pretty soon. Jade Jagger is there. Bear knows her because she did a semester at the Memphis Academy of Art the year before. If you are young and pretty and even remotely famous in Memphis, in those days, Bear knew you.

I get a plate full of red beans and rice and a cold Beck's, chit-chat with Bear and Jade and a couple of her friends about art and fashion and traveling around the world, and how it's going to be for her living in Paris for the next year, and I think to myself, "What a world these people live in." What a total, willful fantasy life they construct for themselves, moving among, interacting with, but never truly living the life inhabited by almost anyone they meet outside the inner circle. Even though several dozen people like me and Bear come into that circle on any given night, we all go back to something very, very different the next day, while this life, this Voodoo Lounge, gets packed up and taken to another stop on the tour, where a new set of white minivans will take everyone from the airport to the Ritz-Carlton, and to the venue and back. The food will be good, and the drinks will be free, and the people hanging on and wishing they were in that life will resemble each other in so many ways.

And I realize in that moment there's no chance in God's creation Jade Jagger will ever remember having met me. I look around and we all notice at the same time we are the last ones in the room. The lights on the stage have gone dark and the rumblings of the throng in the arena begin to crescendo.

It's time to rock and roll.

boomboomboomboomboomboomboomboomboom

The midwife said everything looks and sounds just great—as we have heard with each visit and consultation—and so we keep trucking along, hoping, praying you will get here safe and sound. But we're not simply resorting to acts of faith. Your mom, especially, is eating as well and as much as she has the appetite for: Whole grains, organic fruits and vegetables, very little meat (right now), lots of fresh spring water. And she gets good exercise, too, walking all over our neighborhood with our beautiful dog, a thirteen-year-old Afghan hound named Reggie.

Sometimes she feels a little sick to her stomach, or tired, and she's been very good about taking it easy when she can, lying down for naps most every afternoon. So, we both feel you're getting the best prenatal nutrition and environment we can provide.

Things are also moving along with our attempt to buy the building. We're in contract and just waiting for escrow to close. I'm not (I guess) what one would call "worried" about our financial picture as you are about to be born, but my mind has never been as preoccupied with thoughts of money—and what it means to have enough of it—as it is right now. When you are born next spring, we will undoubtedly be carrying our greatest debt load ever. But in a way that might seem odd, the entire American economy is based on the freedom to do anything for which one can service the debt incurred by borrowing money to cover the costs.

I may be proven wildly wrong in my assessment of the situation—in which case you will have the advantage of having come from humble circumstances—but I think we can hang in here until you are about two, then maybe we'll move to a place where it's a little nicer to be a kid and less expensive to be a person.[7]

---

[7] My assessment ended up being *partially* astute. We "hung in there" in that first apartment till sometime in 2002, then moved to a detached, single family home

For now, I'm trying to keep a handle on running my nightclub, a popular little joint known as Nickie's BBQ, which has been supporting your mom and I for almost nine years, along with the modest inheritance I received from your grandfather. The inheritance is almost gone now and I make up for its absence by trying to be disciplined enough to make money trading in the securities and commodities markets. Fortunately, your mom has a good job with a major airline, and her income we can actually count on.

I'm sure a great number of people, most people even, would say I'm irresponsible and should secure a position to give me a regular income, with which I could then budget our life to give you the best advantages possible. But, as you will come to know, I have always gone my own way and I've tried to act more from the heart than from the head in making life choices.

My heart of hearts is in music,[8] where the chances of me ever providing us with a steady income are two: slim and none. But among the great institutions of capitalism are the securities and commodities markets. Through study, experience, and discipline, the ability to take risks, and perhaps, most importantly, the ability to take losses, one can make a

---

with a backyard in a nicer neighborhood—which certainly seemed a boon for us all. But I was making it happen with smoke and mirrors, taking on ever greater amounts of debt, and the implosion of my personal economy would manifest but a few short months before that of the U.S. (and to a somewhat lesser extent, the global economy). Cool thing about the larger economy is governments can print more money and go further into debt in response to economic shocks. I had to choose between declaring bankruptcy and walking away from my own debt. I chose the latter and spent nearly a decade thereafter fighting off creditors and living in a quasi-underground personal exile.

[8] I went to Nashville in early 1999, investing $30,000 to record a full-length album of original music, much of which I wrote before I got there, but it also benefited immeasurably from contributions of the "Nashville Cats" my producer hired to work with us. The record went nowhere, only to ever be heard by a small number of people who love me anyway and didn't need me to provide a talisman with which to express their appreciation of my creativity and my aspirations.

ton of money trading those markets. Time will tell soon enough if we're to count on my market winnings to brighten our financial picture, because my stake is a modest one, and those don't last long without a good skipper on the raging seas of the financial and industrial markets. As I pray for your health and safety, I pray for my own deliverance in the financial course I've chosen.[9]

---

[9]   I would prove to be an abject failure as a securities and commodities trader over the next four years, losing nearly everything I'd built up from nearly fifteen years running a successful business.

SAVE YOURSELF

Some people want to save the planet, some people want to save the view
Some people want to save a penny, some people don t know what to do
Some people want to save their way of life
Some people want to save the whales
Some people want to make just a little more room In somebody elses' jails
Some people want to save their neighbor from the sin of an early grave
Some people don't want to save nothin at all
When there's only one thing to save
Save yourself

Some people want to save a minute when all they have is time
Some people want to save a criminal in spite of the fact of the crime
Some people want to save the status quo
Some people want to save their ass
Some people want to make a memory of a distant, better past
Some people want to save the Black Man Some want to save the Indian
If anybody's gonna get saved at all it s only gonna begin when you
Save yourself

Some people want to save the magic of the flavor of the fountain of youth
Some people want to save the essence of the mind of the long in the tooth
Some people want to save stamps, some people want to save the schools
Some people want to save the Constitution with a different set of rules
Some people want to save the best for last
Some want to save it all
Some people want to save the drive-in, some people want to save the Mall Save yourself

It's the only thing you really can do
Save yourself
Make every one of your dreams
Come true

RUNNING DOWN A DREAM

I got to Nashville the first weekend in February and made my way from the airport through a light snowfall out to Rusty and Carol's place. They live in a comfortable, inviting house on a little piece of land with a nice pool and a big garage for Rusty's motorcycles and vintage cars just outside town, in Ashland City. I was back in Tennessee to record some of my songs and had arranged for Rusty to produce the project at a studio he likes nearby, in Berryhill. I was grateful Rusty and Carol had offered me accommodations because I had agreed to a recording budget quite beyond my actual means, so not having to pay for a hotel room on top of everything else lessened the financial pressure considerably.

The previous December, I had sent Rusty a tape with twenty songs, from which he picked ten or so that he reckoned were candidates for the project. In the meantime, I'd come up with a couple new ones, and landed in Music City with a pretty good idea of how I wanted the record to sound.

There was one problem. Nobody who would play on it had yet heard any of the tunes. The original idea had been for Rusty and I to spend the weekend of my arrival in pre-production, going over arrangements and picking a definitive list of songs we would then present to the band on Monday morning. I was a little leery of this approach, but Rusty assured me every one of these guys had killer chops and nailing my tunes would be no problem for them.

Little did I know.

Saturday went by with me getting comfortable at Club Rusty. I didn't know him well and had never met Carol—I'd only been introduced to Rusty through a mutual friend while visiting family in Tennessee the preceding Thanksgiving—so the three of us spent time talking about this and that, how each of us came to be sitting there in their living room in front of a crackling fire, amused by the antics of their big ol' German Shepherd, Foote, and their three cats, Astro, Winston, and Naomi.

I worried a little that Rusty and I never seemed to get to talking about the songs, but I figured Sunday might give us time to map out a game plan for the tracking sessions. Saturday night I hardly slept at all, though not for any discomfort with the surroundings; I was simply too excited for sleep.

We enjoyed a lazy Sunday breakfast and during the afternoon, I found myself engrossed in a special on The Nashville Network about players in the pits of NASCAR racing. Stock-car racing is one of Rusty's favorite things, and I enjoyed learning about something I'd never given much thought to before.

As the day got on and we still paid no attention to my songs, I started getting antsy. Rusty finally took my hint and we got the tape out. We grabbed a couple of guitars from Rusty's office, set up a little tape recorder on the living room table and began working on the arrangement for *Mighty Long Way.*

The song is a celebration of everything I've learned and accomplished in life, wrapped in a lament about how satisfaction and happiness still seem out-of-reach. As we started feeling out the changes of the first chorus, I could tell Rusty wasn't into it. He suggested going into the studio cold the next morning, where I could just play the songs for the guys and they could pick 'em right up, and we'd be off and running.

I couldn't believe it. Having been in several bands over the ten or twelve years I'd been making music, all I could think of were memories of struggling for weeks trying to get a song down. Now, here was Rusty suggesting four guys who had never heard my music at all were going to walk in and play ten or twelve songs in a matter of two days. Not only that, but nail them well enough for me to feel good about dropping six months' salary to record them.

I didn't sleep too well Sunday night either, and it wasn't because I was excited. I was scared to death and feared I was in way over my head.

Twenty minutes into Monday at the studio, my fears evaporated like so much dew in the morning sun.

Rusty's *A-Team* welcomed me with big smiles, exuding warm affection that made me feel, somehow, everything really was going to work out. The guys got into their places, tuning instruments and checking sound levels, and Pat, the guitar player, warmed up on a blues riff. I began thinking of a song on my list—*Jamie's in the Doghouse*—and I took off on the vocal. Soon, the others kicked in and we were rocking. It seemed to work. I started feeling better.

We kicked off recording with *Mighty Long Way*. I had the melody pretty well set and played an arrangement that had served me well on solo guitar, but as Rusty had predicted, the fellers had great suggestions for tightening up the bridge and giving the song a more complete feel. We cut the basic track in two takes. Half an hour into Day One, I was having fun, and we were ready for the next tune.

The two tracking days went by in a blur. In one sense, I felt run over by a truck, the way these Nashville Cats took my songs and tweaked and wailed on them mercilessly. The refrain of Melanie's *Look What They Done to My Song, Ma* came to mind more than once... But I also felt embraced and accepted. I thrilled to see and feel the band open themselves to the songs and felt gratified by their contributions to my music.

The free-flowing attitude in the studio obviously owed a lot to these guys' having worked together before. After all, this was Nashville, where making music is notoriously systematic. Guys like these are regularly booked at one of the hundreds of studios in town for eight hour shifts, where they just show up, plug in, and let 'er rip. Rusty and the drummer, Greg, know each other and worked together for years. Greg and the keyboard player, Tony, are co-owners of the studio, so we were on their home turf. Pat and Rusty had forged a kind of creative partnership in the short space of time since Rusty and Carol made the move to Nashville, and along with the bass player, Doug, they had all crossed paths as players on the Nashville studio scene, so everyone was comfortable and easygoing with one another.

Tony came out of his keyboard sanctum to lay down an accordion solo on *Give It Away*, a tune about not holding on so tight during life's sometimes unpredictable ride. Otherwise we didn't see much of him except in the control room, where he patiently mapped out charts for the band while I played the rudiments of each song on an acoustic guitar. Everyone would then make suggestions before assuming positions in the studio's various isolation rooms—and we'd proceed to commit rock and roll.

Anything built in this world is only as strong as its foundation—the principle applies to construction of all kinds, and my project was no different: Fine craftsmen (among music's highest order, in my opinion) coming together for a couple of days to build real-live song parts out of my musical and lyrical sketches and ideas. Many artists and daydreamers must do the same all over the world every day, yet I've heard many-a-tale of woe and disappointment come out of this kind of project.

I originally knew Greg as the drummer in the Memphis band *Larry Raspberry & the Highsteppers*, and felt throughout the many band and concert situations I had seen him play in the Seventies and Eighties, Greg is one of the best rock drummers ever. Nashville made that discovery five or six years ago and today he's one of the most sought-after drummers in the world.

I'm not shitting you. You'll find his name in the credits on a lot of hit records these days and for good reason: the dude rocks. He played drums in the band I hired to play my wedding eight years ago and made them sound like the greatest R&B band ever.

If Greg's solid work on the drum kit forms the foundation of the material, Doug's bass playing is the mortar flowing through it all, binding the various parts together, giving it a solid bottom and a flexible feel. Rusty, multi-instrumentalist that he is, admits to considering himself foremost a bass player, and he's been known to play bass on many of the sessions he's produced over the years. But as we were mixing these songs later, at the end of March, he told me, "I'll never play bass again on a session if Doug's available. I just *love* his bass playing."

59

On overdub day, I saw what it takes to make a rock and roll record. It was just me and Pat and Rusty in the studio that day and we set up Pat's gear in the guitar room while the three of us hunkered down at the board in the control room. Pat picked and chose from his bottomless bag of tricks and toys to find the right tone and nastiness for each cut. In a photo from the sessions you can see Pat's main amps, a vintage Vox AC-30, pre-CBS Fender Deluxe Reverb, an extremely rare 20-watt Marshall head, and if you look real close you can see the tiny little Marshall practice amp we used to get the ur-nasty rhythm tone on *Casey*.

One of the coolest things about making this record was Pat & Rusty's willingness to go for the unexpected, the unusual, the odd—the "wrong" and jarring idea or sound.

As a result, we employed toys like the little Marshall, dimestore guitars like a Western Auto special, and funky sound samples like the "James Bond strings" you can hear in the outro on *Little Bit*.

I'm pretty partial to the driving rock and roll Pat kicks out on *Casey* and *Jamie*, but most of all, I have to admit to tears when he laid down what you hear on *Save Yourself*. He stood there in front of the board in the control room, gorgeous white stratocaster in his hands, and just ripped that song for all it's worth.

That song is a heartfelt rumination on the ways we devote energy to civic projects and great causes in this life but—until each and every one of us gets our own house in order—it's all a lot of wheel-spinning and noise-making. Mr. B dug deep into the reserves of all he's got to give me exactly what the song needed. And witnessing that made me cry.

Then there's Rusty. I can't say enough good things about working with him. Opinionated, crusty, stubborn, moody—he's all that. But he's kind, generous, dependable, and willing to experiment, too. Rusty takes chances despite what convention, tradition, or correctness might call for. He lets everybody do their own thing, encourages each player to do whatever it is they do best, and yet somehow, he gets what *he* wants out of each performance. Rusty contributed a lot of the acoustic guitar, all the percussion, and along with Pat in their incarnation as "The Blend Brothers," backing vocals on *Can't Do Without You, Little Bit,* and *Save Yourself.*

What did I do on this record? Try to stay out of the way, mostly. I was not only my own label executive, paying for the time and talent of professionals, trying to create a vehicle for my skills as a songwriter and singer, I'd also enrolled in a course of education on what it takes to make a real record. I had only been involved in three bona-fide recording projects prior to my experience at Hum Depot, so I came to Rusty and the boys pretty green. They beat me up, and slapped me around in a brotherly way, but they also put the Love Thing on me. I learned a lot with those boys in Tennessee.

I asked questions when they came to me, threw out my ideas and opinions more confidently as time went by, and tried to keep my eyes and ears open to the details and little things that like to sneak in under the radar of common awareness.

I did my best to sing my ass off when the time came. We cut vocals for eleven songs in three days, so I didn't have luxurious amount of time to get things right. Rusty said he was real proud of me after my singing on the first day, but I felt the laborious and frustrating process the isolation of the studio imparts. He took a hands-off approach with me, though he had to remind me to "pretend like [I'm] from Memphis" a few times. He certainly didn't dress my mixes with a lot of fancy effects, so what you hear vocally is pretty pure, uncut me.

All of that said, it's difficult for me to listen to a recording of my own voice. And I imagine sometimes the frightening implications of that for the listener who comes to the music from a place less intimate with it than mine.

NOVEMBER 14, 1999

As you can see, it's been almost a month-and-a-half since I wrote to you last. It's certainly not that you haven't been in my thoughts and prayers, for you are there every day. Your mom had a visit with Judith last week and everything still seems to be fine. Your heartbeat remains strong. In the coming week we will go for an amniocentesis, a procedure by which the doctor inserts a long needle through your mom's belly into the universe where you are growing, the amniotic sac. Some amniotic fluid is drawn out and sent to a laboratory, where it is examined for evidence of any genetic defects or chromosomal abnormalities which might indicate you might have a difficult life in this world.

Even if you are born completely healthy and "normal," life will be difficult for you—it is for all of us. But we are concerned, because of your mom's age, you could have genetic problems that could make your life especially painful and hard to manage. So we are both nervous and hopeful this week's test comes out well. Then, as I've been telling my friends, I can turn my attention to being merely scared to death.

I must admit, as I sit here now, four-and-a-half months prior to your due date, I'm afraid your mother and I may not be married much longer. We have been struggling mightily with issues having to do with our differences as people. We have very strong differences in temperament and in our outlooks on life. We are different in the ways we approach daily tasks of living and in our views of the path to the future. It's stuff that's been there all along in the eleven years we've been together but it's coming to a head now—partly as a result of your impending arrival and partly because that's just the way it is.

No one is right or wrong about the way they are or the way they approach life's challenges, so it isn't a matter of placing blame or responsibility on one or the other of us. The fact is we are both responsible and because we are not communicating effectively right now, I'm afraid the prospects for the future of our marriage do not look bright. This makes me inexpressibly sad. Your mom is angry and afraid, and her thoughts and actions are guided by those powerful emotions. Until she's able to let go of her anger and face her fears, we will not be able to meet on common ground to map a way through and around our differences. So now, we fight. Or we just don't talk at all.

I'm so, so sad and sorry this is how things are, but I believe in my heart everything happens for the best, even when it appears at first glance to be sad, or horrible, or tragic. So I have this great sadness in my heart but I also have great hopes for you and for the world into which you are coming soon. I've been thinking a lot about many things and I know I should set down in print my assessment of myself in all this. It's a hard exercise but I do it as much for my own understanding as in an attempt to let you know me. I have nearly always felt inadequate. I have felt I am not good enough, not sufficient, in other's eyes. Strangely, this feeling hasn't made me try to be as "good" as I can be, in a moral or ethical sense, but rather, I've tried to do and be as much as I can, to do and be more than I really am. I have been extraordinarily adventurous and devil-may-care, for example, so I might be seen and appreciated as something more than just an average guy, more than just a normal human being.

I feel a strong need to be liked, to be thought of as a good person, a nice person, someone you would want to be your friend, or your son, or your husband. As a result of this need, I have not always been truthful with people. When my fear of being disliked or seen as "bad" has come into conflict with an opportunity to tell the truth, I've been influenced by that strong need to "look good," that need to "belong"—and I have lied to people, or hidden the truth so they might "like" me.

This dynamic has gotten me into trouble and caused me untold problems over the years. It forms the whole of my part in the difficulties your mom and I are experiencing now.

I remember lying, and feeling shame over it, when I was 3 or 4. Looking back, I'm sure it was defensive. I didn't want anyone, least of all those closest to me, to think I was "bad." I didn't want to be disliked, or excluded—but most of all, I didn't want anyone to know I wasn't sure what I was doing. Often enough, telling a lie seemed like a way to avoid being exposed. Deep in my consciousness I've understood this fundamental flaw in my makeup, but I've never faced it as clearly and as squarely as I face it now.

Earlier this fall, I was visiting a friend in Boston and I met a woman at a bar. She, too, is married but we felt a spark between us and though we did not fool around physically that evening, we began an extensive, passionate correspondence over email in the succeeding weeks.[10] As

---

[10]   Twenty years on, millions of people all over the world will be using the Internet to search for love and affection—or sometimes—for just an opportunity to get

such things are wont to do, this correspondence became all-consuming. I was constantly distracted by things I was writing to her and by those she was sending to me and soon enough, your mom began to suspect something more than our normal disaffection was at play.

She confronted me. I lied. I told her I was distracted by work. But she didn't believe me and one night, while I was at the club, she went onto my computer and discovered all the correspondence between me and the woman in Boston. I was exposed. And mad. Your mom had betrayed me, going on to my computer and finding things I did not want her to find.

Ahh, but as I said earlier, I believe things happen for the best. And really, whose betrayal was greater?

So, now it's all out in the open. And she is pissed. But you are on the way, and I love your mom. The sparky woman in Boston doesn't mean anything to me—she represents an outlet for thoughts and feelings your mom and I have not paid attention to in too long, and we have an opportunity now to confront those things. We can try and resolve them. Facing this frightens me. At the same time, it's empowering and exciting because I can finally face myself and my future, knowing what I need to know, knowing what I need to do, in order to be the loving, compassionate, happy person I want to be.[11]

---

laid, using "apps" with names like *OK, Cupid* and *Tinder* and *SnapChat.* No app like those existed in the fall of 1999. In the pandemic years of 2020-2021, you yourself will develop a "virtual" friendship with a girl you will meet playing an online game together.

[11] We went fairly immediately into couples' therapy, which shortly came to include individual therapy as well. I felt able to get clear on what I wanted, on who I wanted to be. I wanted to stay married, to have a family and be a full-time father. I committed myself to that vision, though, ultimately, I proved unable to realize it.

NOVEMBER 20, 1999

Yesterday was a big day. Your mom went in for the amniocentesis and everything went smoothly. In two weeks or so we'll get the test results back, so there's still some nervousness involved for both of us, but at least the procedure itself went well. We got some more pictures via ultrasound and you are coming right along. We saw your spinal column very clearly, and your hands and feet. In one picture, it looks like you are giving a "thumbs up" sign, in our culture a traditional signal that all is well.

The doctor said your heartbeat continues to be very strong and the size of your head and body seems right in line with normal development. So everything with you is just fine.

Your mother and I are still not seeing eye-to-eye. She's very, very angry with me. I have a feeling we may not live together when you are growing up. But who knows? It's still several months before you even come to meet us and many things can happen in that amount of time. So, I'm sad, but hopeful, too. I hope you will one day know deep in your heart and soul how much I love you.

DECEMBER 15, 1999

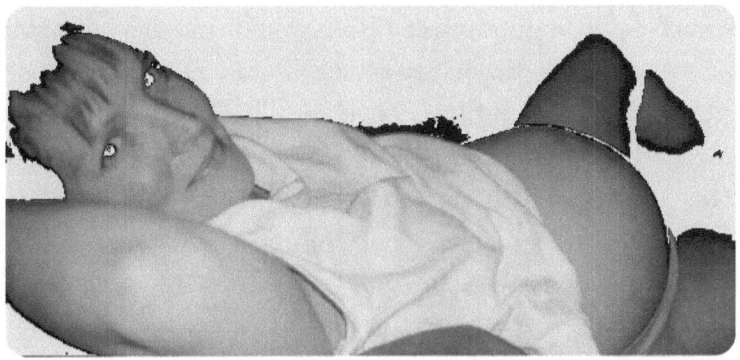

t's been a few weeks since I've had a chance to sit down and write some more, so I guess I should mention first off the amnio results were excellent. Your chromosomes are all in line, and your cellular structure seems a fine foundation on which to develop a life in this world. Hooray! We both have breathed many sighs of relief over the good news, though we continue to appreciate the possible problems and potential difficulties that lie ahead. And I guess now is as good a time as any to begin anticipating some of the questions you are going to have for us.

- Is there a God?
- Who is God?
- What is Heaven?
- Hell?
- What happens when we die?
- Why are we here?
- Why do bad things happen to some people and why do good things happen to others?
- How can I be sure what is right and what is wrong?

Everyone struggles with many of the same questions and uncertainties, and the ways people answer those questions, and their strategies for dealing with those uncertainties, define the various cultures and societies you will find in your time here.

On the surface, it might appear different cultures have dramatically differing views of life, but in my own relatively short time observing and experiencing the rich diversity of people in this world, I've come to appreciate how similar are our approaches to some of the greatest mysteries. Everyone confronts these questions and they do not necessarily have immutable answers. The answers that end up working for you will be the ones you discover for yourself.

Try always to remember this: the Universe contains everything you need to know. It will reveal its true nature if you seek to find it. Should you undertake the search, I guarantee you will be amazed and overjoyed at what an incredible thing the Universe is.

I believe you have chosen me and your mom to bring you back into this world.[12]

Yes, you have been here before. I believe we all go through multiple lifetimes in our search for the truth and for the way back to our original birthplace, the mind of God, which people call Heaven.

It takes many lifetimes because *the way* is difficult and people are not often strong enough to make the journey in any one lifetime. There

---

[12] This, of course, is by no means a universally accepted understanding. I merely express to you my own belief. I will go on to try and introduce you to mindfulness practice, meditation, and yoga in your early teen years and you will reject them all. We will have discussions about God and spirituality and you will seem to land squarely in the atheist camp, expressing a belief that everything that's here is all there is. You will not turn out to be a nihilist, however, not before your 20s, anyway, and so I suspect there may still be room for you to attain something of a belief in spirituality and an understanding that we do have agency in creating the nature of the life we inhabit.

are many lessons to learn and when we don't learn all the lessons in a particular lifetime, after we die, we come back to learn the ones we missed before. With each lifetime, we try and make a little more progress on the path until, eventually, we understand and live in the complete truth of the Universe. Then we no longer have to return to life in human form.

So, yes, I believe you have chosen us to bring you into this life to guide you on your way to discovering the truth. And you are very smart, I already know, because you have chosen two people who have worked hard in our lives to find our own truths. Your mom and I are both excited about helping you discover your way on the path to Heaven, or Nibbana, or whatever may lie beyond this life.

DECEMBER 29, 1999—JAÈN, SPAIN

Beyond the rolling plains of Andalusia in southern Spain, tucked among the Sierra Nevada foothills north of Granada, a fine Arab fortress from the thirteenth century crowns a rocky outcropping. For hundreds of years, the fortress served as a strategic haven and stronghold, controlling access to the long valley whose view it commands.

For a brief, shining moment, it was ours. From December 29, 1999 until January 2, 2000, the fortress and the unsuspecting town over which it keeps silent watch endured a siege the likes of which it hasn't seen since the middle of the first half of the last millennium. Where past assaults and defenses of the battlements at this glorious medieval site held great riches and vast tracts of land in the balance of their outcomes, our band of nearly sixty adults and eight kids were merely treated to one of the great New Years–New Millennium celebrations we've heard of.

72

The schedule (from a website I created to sell the package tour to anyone beyond our relatively small circle of friends who might come across it):

Millennium Bill of Fare

DECEMBER 29
Arrival at the Parador Castillo de Santa Catalina.
Welcome gala this evening at the Parador, including a cocktail party with a delicious selection of Spain's famous TAPAS (hot & cold hors d'oeuvres) and open bar. During the cocktail hour, a local regional folkloric dance troupe or a "Tuna" (medieval minstrels) will perform for the guests. Welcome dinner of Spanish specialties, including regional wines. After dinner enjoy a Flamenco guitar and song exhibition by talented local artists.

DECEMBER 30 Buffet breakfast.
Today features an optional full day tour to Granada, including the famed Alhambra, once the pleasure palace and fortress of Arab caliphs, and to nearby Sacromonte Gypsy Caves, including lunch with regional wines. (Optional tours are not included in the package price). This evening will feature a special Medieval Banquet at the Parador, hosted by the Count and Countess of the castle, featuring a troubadour, court jester and waiters dressed in medieval garb. These local actors will sit and mingle with the guests in what will surely be a night to remember. Wine will flow freely.

DECEMBER 31 Buffet breakfast.
Today's optional morning tour will be of Jaen and will feature the Roman baths and the Museum of Iberian Art. Lunch at the Parador. Afternoon free. Tonight's special "End of Century/New Year's Dinner Bash" at the Parador will feature a sumptuous 4-course dinner, featuring Rioja wines, beer and "Cava" (champagne), plus a 5-piece band for dancing until 2AM. At midnight a spectacular fireworks display from the battlements of the castle will bring in the new millennium in stellar fashion.

JANUARY 01 Buffet breakfast.
Morning at leisure. Perhaps stroll along the castle walls, taking in the first view of the new millennium over the seemingly endless vista of olive groves. At mid-morning our Chef, Mr. Miguel Marabe Garcia, will be giving a complimentary cooking class on typical Andalusian Cuisine where the culinarily inclined may learn the taste secrets of the delicious local food. Lunch at the Parador. Today's optional afternoon tour will be

to ancient Cordoba, featuring the famed Great Mosque (now a cathedral), with its labyrinth of columns and charming Jewish Quarter. Tonight's farewell dinner party at the Parador will be followed by an Andalusian Fiesta, featuring a Flamenco dance troupe performing typical dances such as sevillanas, rumbas and colombianas - audience participation is encouraged. At tonight's farewell dinner, a special commemorative end-of-century ceramic, by local artist Paco Tito, will be given to each guest as a special souvenir of this event.

JANUARY 02 Buffet breakfast. End of services.

The main event, outside of the New Year's gala itself, was a Medieval Banquet on the night of the 30th. Given the grandeur of the setting, it seemed befitting we begin our celebrations in earnest with a costume ball. After all, we'd been invited by the Count and Countess of the castle to a reception and dinner in the Grand Ballroom the night before New Years Eve, where they promised entertainment with skits and dancing provided by the Court Troubadour and a band of local actors. So our group decided to join in the fun. We outfitted ourselves in raiments recalling a bygone age of elegance and intrigue, and joined the castle royals for a truly magical night of unbridled merrymaking.

After the Count & Countess made their grand entrance, we found our way to the dining hall, where the Count welcomed us with a gracious speech and laid before us the protocol for the evening's events. There seemed an undercurrent of tension between the two royals, an air of suspicion infusing their relationships with other members of the court. In particular, something appeared to be going on between the Count and the Gypsy Fortuneteller, and between the Countess and the Troubadour. This instability at court led a few instigators in our party to hatch a plan for a palace coup.

It took a while, because our hosts were doing their best to fête and entertain us, but eventually Lord Brian of Baltimore and Marcus Rahim, visiting moorish dignitary from the Potomac Basin, enlisted the Troubadour in a brutal plan to oust the Count and install Duke

Theo of the Bonederosa as titular head of the Castillo and its vast holdings.

The Count struck us as the nervous type from the very beginning. He'd made a show of demanding Doc, the Eastside High-Stepper—who was busy working his magic on the gypsy fortune teller—reveal the contents under his big hat. When it was clear no offending weaponry was concealed thereby, the Count seemed only a little placated. He soon designated Akmed el D, Sultan of Magaña Batiste, to be his personal taster. This tended to draw the evening out, as there were several courses on the menu and a variety of offerings in each course. But the Sultan was happy to oblige. He enjoyed the extra portions of Black Sausage, Leek & Onion Stew, Marinated River Fishes, Veal Stew, and Roast Kid, all the while giving the conspirators time to formulate strategy for carrying out their nefarious deed.

One wonders how an impromptu coup could be arranged under the noses of such a public audience and a wary victim, but the Count was distracted by his jealousy of the cat in the hat, while the Countess seemed only too pleased by the chance of having her philandering Count done away with. The rest of the party was frankly too concerned with keeping goblets filled to notice villainy in the air. Then, while the Court Jester and his actors provided a distraction in preparation for one of their entertainments, the usurpers struck.

"There is a *conspiration* in the court!" cried the Count, as Marcus Rahim brandished a gleaming dagger. The Troubadour and Lord Jimmy of the Bottomless Cup overpowered the hapless Count with help from Duke Theo, and hustled him shrieking from the room. The court was stunned. The Countess and the Gypsy feared for their virtue. Lord Brian addressed the company, announcing the ascension of Duke Theo to the throne. And the burly pretender reemerged to sycophantic applause from the assembled revelers.

Where would this tyranny lead? Could the sacrifice of virgins and the slaying of fatted calves be far behind? Duke Theo spoke amid a hushed and nervous silence. No fool he, Duke Theo realized the Count held the keys to the kingdom. Only the rightful Lord of the Manor could speak the language of the chefs and entertainers, and without his continued presence the evening would surely devolve into debauchery, suiting the tastes of a small, though vocal minority.

So, in a grand gesture of reconciliation, The Duke's first act as the new ruler of the castle was to allow the Count to return to the court as a mere citizen, but one who would continue to direct the evening's affairs and see to it our expectations for a magical night remained undimmed. And magic there was aplenty.

In a graphic portrayal of the fickleness of crowds, the court turned on Lord Jimmy when Lord Brian & Marcus Rahim fingered him as the mastermind of what the Count was now calling a "failed coup." Putting it to a thumbs up-thumbs down vote, the Count obtained a resounding call for punishment, with a great pounding of tables and bloodthirsty chants of "Off with his head!" echoing throughout the hall. In the end, he was only forced to consume a strong measure of wine in a single go, which, as Lord of the Bottomless Cup he managed in dramatic, yet effortless fashion.

There were fair maidens and dancing girls, fine skits by the court players, a flamenco guitar interlude, toasts all around. Everyone danced into the wee hours of the morning, gaily, joyously, drunk on the happiness of a feast well-laid. Actually, in the wee hours of the morning some of our revelers appeared drunk on a bit more than just the happiness of a feast well-laid. Impromptu jousting round a stairway above the bar resulted in some smashed pottery and a few tears. One of our company was abducted by local bacchanalians, who paraded him to the bars in town until well past morning light.

The day crew was not pleased with the state of the hall when they came on duty. Only seven of us made the tour of town and the olive oil factory the next day. Yes, there was slight wreckage in the wake of the medieval costume ball, but everyone agreed; it had truly been one for the memoirs.

THE YEAR 2000

January 9

Here we are, in the last year of the twentieth century, the last year of the second millennium since the birth of Jesus Christ. Many people celebrated nine days ago, when the western calendar changed from 1999 to 2000, feeling the new century and the new millennium began then. And I guess it doesn't really matter because the birth of Jesus Christ is such an arbitrary date from which to mark time, in addition to the fact that time itself is a relative concept.

But it *was* a good excuse for a party. I hope you will find, in time, a few good friends who feel as you do about life, and go exploring with them all the many wondrous and exciting places on the planet. There is no place like home, but there is also nothing better than leaving home and going to visit other people in *their* homes, in their countries, to see the way *they* do things, eat the foods they eat, dance to their music, and see the world through their eyes. When you have traveled, it makes coming home something special and gives you a great appreciation of your own people, your own culture, and your own way of being in the world.

Your way of being in your world right now, inside your mom, is apparently quite active. You move around a lot and we are having lots of fun feeling your movements in there. Your mom thinks sometimes it's because you are hungry. Other times, after she's been pretty active for a while, rocking you gently inside your watery universe, you seem to start flipping around when she settles, as in a chair, or lying down to sleep at night. Especially when she lies down to sleep at night.

And I guess now, about six months into your nine-month gestation, you are beginning to be able to hear sounds. So, hopefully you will be soothed by your mom's and my voice when you get here—cause those are the voices you are beginning to hear now. I have to admit, I don't really know what to say to you, though I have this strong urge to say something; I guess it's a manifestation of the anxiety I feel about having you on the way to join us.

We are starting to get ready for you. We were in Amsterdam at the end of our trip last week and spent some time in a baby store there, where we bought you a few of the first outfits you will wear when we take you around and introduce you to everyone. I hope you will like them and find them comfortable. We have also been batting around ideas for what to name you. Up till now we've referred to you as "The baby," "Little One," "It," and sometimes "he" or "she." We don't yet know if you are a boy or a girl; we are going to let you surprise us when you get here. But that makes coming up with a name even harder. We haven't decided for certain yet, but I think we have a couple of strong candidates for a boy or a girl, though it seems like we agree on the girl-name more than we do the boy-name.

I should report, too, that we are doing much better these days. Your mom isn't quite as angry with me as she was several weeks ago and she seems to be better able to deal with her fears too. This morning we meditated together for the first time in forever and spent five minutes looking deeply into each other's eyes at the end of the session. It was wonderful. I think it has made us feel closer to one another and we want to make it a regular part of our practice. So, my hopefulness of a couple of months ago seems not entirely misplaced....

February 3

It's hard to believe a month has gone by since I wrote to you last. But much has happened. We've returned to our routines, your mom to her life working with people at the airport, me to my nightclub business in the city. We meditated together a few times in the last month but I wouldn't say we've made it part of our regular practice yet, and for myself, I've allowed my own meditation practice to become intermittent. It upsets me a little, but I know I will be still and clear again.

Your mom went to an extraordinary event last week. Fourteen pregnant moms got together to share stories of their experience. They discussed their hopes and fears and excitement and joy about the prospect of having a new life coming into their world. Everyone made or brought a different dish of food and they made a whole afternoon of it. It is rare in this society for groups of unrelated people to get together in such a way, though perhaps less so here in California, where people are always trying new ways of being, searching for new ways to get at the truth of what life is all about. I think your mom enjoyed it, and it seems as though we know who your first playmates will be.

I remain close friends with one of my first playmates, your uncle SH, who we affectionately call "Y'Daddy," and who will always steer you right should you lose your way.

I've been inspired to sit at the keyboard tonight because I got a call from your mom, who is out at the airport working. She said she discovered some "spotting" or bleeding, and was concerned there might be a problem. We consulted one of her reference books and got an understanding of what could be going on. As always in such a delicate and precious condition—bringing a new life into being is certainly that—it's a good idea to inform a doctor what is happening. Sometimes the doctor will understand a situation clearly, other conditions may seem harder to diagnose. Caution usually dictates going to see the doctor as soon as possible, unless it is clearly unnecessary. And tonight calls for caution. So your mom is on her way home and we'll be going to the hospital to get an ultrasound look at you and perhaps see what, if anything, might be out of the ordinary. I'm hopeful, yet frightened, too.

February 29

You can see by the time that's passed, we didn't encounter anything too serious at the hospital that night. It's pretty normal for a woman to leak fluids here and there during pregnancy but the doctors wanted to be especially on the safe side, given your mom's age and her history of miscarriage. I can't remember if I mentioned it above, but we had two miscarriages in the past several years before you came along. So you really are something of a miracle baby.

We got a good reading on your heartbeat that night. Very strong and steady. In fact the OB/GYN staff were a little surprised by how strong you sounded in there and they exchanged some knowing glances when they saw the readout on the monitor. We tried to ask them what it all meant, but in keeping with what you will one day discover for yourself as the medical profession's vested interest in keeping patients mystified (and thus beholden to medical professionals in their efforts to treat their ailments and maintain good health), they just told us we didn't have anything to worry about.

Ha! Nothing to worry about, my patootie!

We are both plenty worried about all kinds of things having to do with your impending arrival—I can't believe you are scheduled to be here in eight-and-a-half weeks—most of our worries center around our own uncertainties and feelings of inadequacy as parents-to-be. It's not like we've done this before, nor is there an established manual setting out the best methods for raising a child.

There are plenty of books and courses available on the subject; and every person we meet seems to have pearls of wisdom and sage advice they are willing to give us, even without our asking. Each person and each family presents unique problems. We are all just going to have to do the best we can with the abilities we have at hand.

So, no matter how well or how poorly we manage the tasks of bringing you into this life and preparing you for making your way in it, you should know that we very much want to do a good job, that we very much hope you will come to believe in, and take security and comfort in the depth of the love we both have for you.

Next week we'll begin attending a class at the hospital where you'll be born. The class will give us some idea of what to expect in the labor and delivery process, and give us a foundation in the things we'll need to be aware of during your first weeks and months here. We have already been reading a few books on pregnancy and childrearing and we have a pretty good idea of what is going on with you inside your mom's abdomen. She, of course, can feel your every movement now. And we can both see the changes in the shape of her stomach when you are moving around.

It's very exciting! You are a very active baby, moving and grooving and jumping whenever your mom settles into a chair or lies down to take some rest. The doctors told us we should count the time it takes you to make four kicks every morning when your mom has breakfast. Apparently there is a norm around ten minutes which indicates a healthy baby. You almost always get in your four kicks within half that time!

Now, we have no idea if that means you are half-normal, or some kind of superhero, or what, but we're pretty sure you are strong and healthy, which is about all one can ask for in this life.

March 24

As I sit to type I question whether or not what I feel is "stunned" by today's events. If it means "incapable of action," I am not far from it, judging by how long it's taken me to get through two sentences.

Your mom is in the hospital, has been there since noon today, and it appears very likely you will be coming out to meet us much sooner than we anticipated.

I don't know what to say.

By all appearances we are not "ready" for you: the apartment is a total wreck from being repainted throughout; we haven't even begun to clear out space in my office, dressing room—my sanctuary in a way—to make room for your crib, your dressing table, and all the stuff you'll find when you get here; we don't have your infant car seat yet—it's on order—nor the comfy little crib sheets and bumper set we plan to lie you in to sleep each night.

Right. You sleep each night. I'm sure later in this document I'll have a better perspective for writing about your infant sleep patterns.

Suffice it to say for now we are both feeling weird that we don't have your crib all set up and ready to bring you home to, if you come to us in the next day or two.

You have been a wonderful baby to carry—if I read your mom correctly—and everything about this pregnancy has been right on schedule and right within positive parameters at each of your development milestones. Only in the last several days did she begin complaining of swelling in her feet and hands. We first chalked it up to the warmer weather we've been having the past couple of weeks, and to your mom's job, where she spends a good deal of her time on her feet dealing with passengers at the airport. We looked in one of our reference books and found such swelling is a fairly common occurrence in many pregnancies. But we also found it could be symptomatic of a condition called preeclampsia, in which the mother develops high blood pressure, creating a very dangerous situation for both mother and child.

Years ago, before the medical community began to understand and identify preeclampsia, the mother often died in or shortly after childbirth, and babies were always at risk for being born with very low birth weight and an underdeveloped immune system. Now, although no one really knows what causes preeclampsia, it is easy to identify and doctors know how to deliver a child without presenting a grave risk to the mother.

We called the hospital and told them what was going on. They suggested perhaps your mom should come in and let them check her blood pressure and test her urine for protein, which would indicate preeclampsia in a more advanced stage and require everyone preparing to deliver you in the next day or so.

That was yesterday.

By that point, however, she had begun to feel a little better and decided to wait until this morning and see how she felt before deciding to go to the hospital. We have a little home blood pressure monitor and we used it on both of ourselves after breakfast today. We were both alarmed to see your mom's blood pressure up pretty high. Another call to the hospital and they said definitely come in, which your mom did, and everything has moved pretty fast since then. I left her there a little earlier this evening, where she was resting comfortably with her blood pressure lower and relatively stabilized.

Tomorrow we'll see what happens: maybe she can come home and we'll see you in a couple of weeks; perhaps her blood pressure will re-elevate and we'll have you in a couple of days.

Either way I'm so excited, and strangely not that concerned over the fact your crib isn't set up and we don't yet have all the sweet little sounds and images we want to bring to you in your earliest days here.

I know I have room for you in my life no matter what or who else is in it, and I feel we'll always find comfort in our love, regardless of the comfort in our surroundings. That's it for now, little L. Your heart beats strong. I can't wait to hold you in my arms.

April 7

Thankfully, you've kept us waiting.

Your mom got to come home from the hospital the next day and for the past couple of weeks we've been monitoring her blood pressure. She's been stopping by the hospital every couple of days, where they have checked her out—and you, too, via fetal heart monitor. Everything seems just fine. Just between you and me: there is a certain chemistry between your mom's, shall we say, concerned, inquisitive nature, and the nature of doctors and hospitals to want to practice medicine, which creates a little more drama than might otherwise be called for.

What I'm trying to say is that I think we could have passed the last couple of weeks a little more normally than we did without increasing the stress of our fears and concerns about your birth. Our fears and concerns are natural and understandable, but I think we've allowed ourselves to become distracted by them. Which is neither here nor there, just my venting a little of my own "stuff."

We've also had an opportunity to get the apartment back into some semblance of livability, started putting your nursery together, and I feel we've grown closer to one another, discovered a part of our love we didn't know was there.

Everything really is fine, and we're both so excited to meet you.

It's been extremely beneficial for you to remain in the womb these past couple of weeks. Your lungs have been undergoing their final development and your immune system, the wonderful mechanism of the human body that protects us from disease and helps us recover from sickness and injury, has been in its final stages of development.

In four days, you will have spent thirty-seven weeks growing in your mom's uterus, which the doctors consider enough time to develop fully.

A full-term pregnancy is considered to be forty weeks of gestation, but if you were to come any time now, the doctors tell us you will be born healthy.

These last couple of days your mom has said she can feel your head moving down toward the birth canal, a phase called "lightening" that is said to occur about two weeks prior to birth, which would be really wonderful. We both want you to enjoy the benefits of your time in the womb as long as possible. Now you are in a place where the temperature is perfect, the environment is peaceful and calm, and your every need is taken care of.

You are bathed in the steady rhythm of your mom's heartbeat and rocked in the gentle sway of amniotic waters. You are in for a rude awakening when you get here.

I wrote a song for your mom in the last week, although your presence inspired my thoughts and feelings in a very real way. Perhaps you've heard me singing it to her. You know, it's also said babies can hear music from within the womb and have been known to respond after their birth to songs played for them when they were in utero. I'll be so excited if you seem to respond to my music when you get here...you have no idea.

It feels great to write a love song. And when I see the love in your mom's eyes when I play it for her, I get a feeling I know no way of describing.

I KNOW WHAT LOVE IS

I know what love is
And the way it feels
Like a drug
If it's phony
Like nothing if it's real.
Give me Love over money
Give me Love after all
Give me Love, won't you honey Be the belle of my ball
You don't need to compromise your peace of mind
Now my restless heart has finally found a home
I know I could never find the openhearted kindness
You bring to me
No matter where I roam
Yes, I know what Love is
And the way it feels
And the way I feel for you, it must be Love
The way you make me feel, it must be Love

© 2000 L. Lazar (ASCAP) From the EP "Take Root" by Lonnie Lazar & The Vaporizers

PART 2

VIVA! LOFTON

JUNE 13, 2000

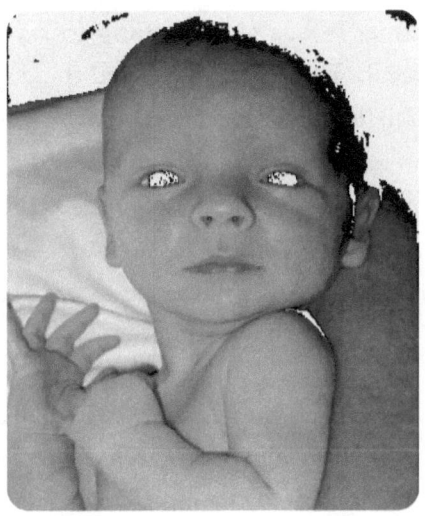

I f I thought I was unsure how to address you in prior installments, now I'm at a total loss!

Here you are, almost two months old and I'm just now getting around to writing again? Only if you ever have children of your own will you understand what the past seven-and-a-half weeks have been like for us.

Suffice it to say time has been in short supply for ruminating at the keyboard on Life's Big Questions.

Lofton, you'll have heard it a million times by the time you read this, but you are the most precious, adorable, wonderful baby who has ever been born. This, of course, is a feeling and a certainty shared by millions of parents toward their own babies the world over on any given day, but somehow I long to convince you, to prove to you, that I mean it more than any of them possibly could mean it about their children.

Alas, I will have to show it to you, to model my appreciation of your magnificence in tangible, memorable ways over the years to come, and I can only hope to be able to retain a sense of this overwhelming love and appreciation once we get into the long, hard slog of living together.

Meanwhile, your name. It was always going to start with L, whether you turned out to be a boy or a girl. We asked the doctors to keep your gender from us pre-birth, a decision for which we both are so glad. The surprise of that moment you were born and the doctor who delivered you cried, "it's a boy!" was so, so delicious. Your mom and I had long settled on "Loretta" if you were to turn out to be a girl but we had been at a great impasse on a boy's name until just a week or two before you arrived.

We had begun to feel good about "Lucas," but when I couldn't promise not to call you "Luke" for short, she nixed the Lucas idea. I don't remember exactly how it came to me but I suggested "Lofton" one day and your mom beamed, because Lofton was the name of her maternal grandfather, a man she loved as a little girl, and I felt it was a nice way of thanking her for permitting us to use L, given that is the letter of my own first name.

Once we got there, there was no going back. It's an unusual first name, it's a family name, and now that you're here, I could never imagine naming you anything but.

Viva Lofton!

JULY 23

I t's 3:45 a.m. I've just come home from one more Saturday night at Nickie's.

We were crowded tonight and the music was good. People danced and drank and laughed and had a real good time. Nights like tonight make me happy to own a nightclub. They can be few and far between, though, and as I approach my fortieth birthday in a couple of weeks, I have a difficult time seeing myself involved in the bar/nightclub business much longer.

Trouble is, I have no idea what I can see myself involved in, other than in the challenge of raising you, providing for your physical, emotional, spiritual sustenance until you are able to make your own way in the world.

I had a pretty good year trading stocks and commodities last year, which gives me hope I can generate income that way in years to come. But as for becoming involved in another business after Nickie's, I just don't know. All I do know is I don't want to run Nickie's much longer.

You are three months old now and just the most precious, adorable little guy. You seem quite content as a general rule, are happy and gleeful throughout the day; calm, alert, and peaceful as you wind yourself down to sleep each night.

I was going to write about what a good sleeper you've been, but tonight you woke crying for the first time in many weeks. Your Mom got up and fixed a bottle, which I then fed to you. I've just laid you back down to sleep and it's now after 4:30 a.m., so I will bid you goodnight and write again when I can.

JULY 29

Seems these 3:30 a.m. rendezvous are proving to be the only times I have to make new entries into what I've dubbed the Baby Journal.

As I write, I have no idea when I might give this document to you: when you are ten? When you're a teen? When you go to college? After I die?[13]

Which doesn't really matter, I guess, because I'm not writing to a future you.[14] I am writing to you, who is sleeping contentedly not ten feet away from me in the next room.

You are beginning to come to terms with the fact that you are in physical space, that you have hands and feet, arms, and legs, and you are starting to let us know your consciousness is rising through little smiles, glints in your eyes, and all manner of wonderful sounds you make. If you've been fed and had your diaper changed, you can lie in your crib or your changing table, or on the play mat your grandmother Lore gave to you, for twenty, thirty, forty-five minutes at a time during the day. Your Mom and I love to watch you at play with the mobiles over the crib and the changing table, and we find it comforting to have you in view as you screech and yelp, batting and kicking at the little hanging toys on the play mat.

---

[13] Happy 21st birthday.

[14] Look, it's a crack in the time-space continuum. Who is reading this now?

OCTOBER 29

I t's 9:00 a.m. on a beautiful—bright, crisp, and clear—Sunday morning. Your mom sleeps soundly in our bed, resting comfortably after her first night back to work since before you were born. Seven months she's been off, the three of us spending almost all of that time together, forming the bonds on which our lives as a family will forever depend.

You are snoozing in your car seat, perched with the warm sun to your back on the dining room table, taking your first nap of the day. We got up at a little after 6:00 a.m. to the sound of a ringing telephone and your annoyed cries at the disturbance. Whoever it was didn't leave a message. Your Mom got up and brought you from your crib into our bed, where we played for a while. Well, you played; we let you pull our hair, poke your fingers into our eyes and noses, kick us in the chest with your powerful little legs, cooing, laughing, and blowing bubbles with your tongue until I got up to make you a bottle, which your mom fed you while I took Reggie outside for her morning walk.

When we got back I came to take you from your mom so she could go back to sleep, and you and I adjourned to the living room, where the morning sun bathed everything in a soft, warm light.

You are so very observant of your environment. Calm yet inquisitive about surprisingly more than whatever is simply right in front of you— all infants are adept at contemplating their navels. But you truly give us a sense of being aware of the wider world, of the horizon beyond your immediate gaze. Of course, I could be projecting my own dream of you.

I make as conscious an effort as I can to be aware that you are not my expectations of you. Still, you amaze and delight me to no end.

So, we played for a bit together on the couch, then you let me put you on the floor with a couple of your toys and I read part of the morning paper while you rolled around, giggling and laughing to yourself, looking up to me just every now and again to make sure I was paying attention.

At six months, you are in the embryonic stages of mobility. You can sit up unassisted, push yourself up very strongly into what you'll come to know as an "upward dog" yoga pose or *chadarandasana*, roll over back-to-front, front-to-back with ease, and scoot on your hands and knees, though, at this point, only backwards. We can tell you really want to go forward sometimes, but you haven't figured out the hand/knee balance equation yet.

Soon your Mom and I will be scurrying around the apartment, "baby-proofing" it, as the term has come to be known, so you won't be in danger of hurting or killing yourself as you get more mobile and strong, and thus, more likely to get beyond our field of vision.

Perhaps I'll return to this topic next time, but now I hear you stirring from your slumber and I'm certain there is a dirty diaper to be changed before we head to the kitchen for breakfast. You just gave me a good forty minutes of quiet time; thank you, Lofton.

DECEMBER 25

Your first Christmas.

Today was a beautiful day here. Clear skies, crisp temperatures—you, your mom, I, and Reggie, The Hall of Fame Dog, went for a nice long walk in the neighborhood after we opened our presents. You were far more interested in the wrapping paper and ribbons than you were in the contents of any particular gift, a bit of here-and-now consciousness I'll have to remember to appreciate as your taste for material diversions grows in the years to come.

As always, I don't really have much time to write. There are far too many logistical necessities yet undone. Reggie must still be walked, the garbage bagged and put out; the kitchen must be straightened up; and you will still need a diaper change and a bottle before the night can wind down for your mom and me. By the time all those logistics are attended to, you will be in your nursery, shared with the computer on which I write this memoir, sleeping soundly, providing all the barrier I need to keep me from sitting down to write to you more.

I did, however, want to mark this occasion—when friends and family the world over exchange gifts in honor and celebration of the birth of Jesus Christ—to let you know your mom and I feel you are the greatest gift we could ever have.

2001

April 21

Y ou can tell by the nearly four months that have passed since I wrote last—it has been a busy year. I've been keeping a little daily journal on a separate calendar, recording the things we've all been doing, listing your developmental milestones, noting the people, places, and events we've all been experiencing in your first year of life. But I really have not had time to sit down and write to you in this journal the way I've wanted to.

Today is your first birthday and, looking back on the year, it seems to have passed very quickly. At any particular point in time during the year, if you'd asked, I would not have said time appeared to be moving quickly at all.

There are issues of time and relativity you will one day come to understand, though perhaps never quite as well as you will understand them if (when?) you have your own children. Children are always "in the moment" and adults are often, in our minds, anyway, thinking about something in the past or planning for something in the future. I try to be in the moment with you as much as I can.

Today happened to fall on a Saturday, which is a big work day in your mom's schedule, and so you and I had the day almost all to ourselves. I took you to Pac Bell Park and we watched the San Francisco Giants play baseball against the Milwaukee Brewers.

It was a gorgeous day and you enjoyed yourself immensely. We took a photograph out in the center field bleachers and you fell asleep drinking a nice big bottle of milk during the seventh inning.

I love the way you enjoy going out and seeing and doing new things. You have no fear of people and everyone finds you adorable and charming. It brings me great pride and joy.

Because I worked last night at Nickie's until 3:00 a.m. and had to go back down there this morning at 8:00 a.m. to meet some workmen who were doing some repair work, I am quite sleep-deprived and am just about falling asleep at the keyboard even as I type this. But I could not let your birthday pass without making an entry.

Your mom and I are more in love with you every day. You are so smart, so happy, so fun to be around—although you are a great challenge to us both. You require lots of attention and your needs are very demanding on our time, our patience, our energy, and on our imagination but it is all very much worth it because you return to us so much more than we give to you.

We continue to think of you as a great blessing in our lives. And we have grown closer to one another as you have grown, too. We have been reminded of the reasons we fell in love with one another and, although we still have our very deep-seated differences, we have begun to respect and appreciate one another much more than we did in the months before you were born.

Our little house is a happy home and that is reflected in your sunny disposition. So, all in all, here on the eve of your second year of life, everything seems very, very right.

Thank you again, Lofton, for choosing us, and for bringing your light into our lives. I can only hope we are able to communicate to you what a great gift your presence is in this world and to instill in you an understanding and an appreciation for what that means to us, to you, and to the world you will inherit and act upon as you go through life. I know we are both really looking forward to the next year of your development, no matter how tired we may end up growing as we try to keep up with you and spur you on to the greatness of which you are surely capable.

May 12

Today you and I went to Berkeley to meet my friend SG and his daughter Rose, who is a couple of years older than you.

We made stops at the bank and the post office before getting into the flow of traffic bound eastward over the Bay Bridge. I like to joke with my old friend, who lived for many years in San Francisco, about the supposed inferiority of life in the East Bay, chiding him for taking a step down in leaving "everybody's favorite city."

The fact is, in many ways, life in the East Bay may be superior to life in the City, not in the least of which is the weather. San Francisco is bloody cold much of the time.

The one thing that could keep me from ever moving over there, however, is the traffic. Far too many vehicles and far too much dependence on use of the freeway to get around the east bay for my taste. But we braved the bridge traffic today and went shopping on 4th street, both S and I pushing Rose and you in your strollers, two dads out shopping with their kids the Saturday before Mothers 'Day. Rose was asleep in her stroller most of the time, but you had slept for an hour and twenty minutes in the car before we got to Berkeley, so you were quite interested in all the stuff going on in the stores and on the sidewalks outside.

We stopped for pizza, for which Rose woke up, and then we tried to find a camera to give to your mom for Mothers 'Day, but the shops we went to didn't have what I wanted. It was great seeing our friends, but soon time came for us to say our farewells and hit the bridge again for the return home.

We stopped at Nickie's to get a few things done and by the time we got home it was already after 7:00 p.m. Too much time in the car, as I said, but it was good to get you out for a little road trip and to see a new place. You saw your first train close up today, and seemed to like the bell and the whistle. Tonight you had fun playing in the bathtub and after almost finishing a 6 oz. bottle of milk lying in my arms, you dozed quietly to sleep at 8:39 p.m. It's now three hours later and you are still sleeping peacefully.

It turns out, you have been one of the all-time champion sleeping babies, almost from the very beginning.

Some people cannot stand to hear about it—most of them are parents with infants of their own—but I tell 'em you've been sleeping through the night since you were five weeks old. And it's pretty darn close to the truth. Some nights you may stir around midnight, others, two or four in the morning, but we don't take you out of your crib and you always fall back asleep once you know one of us is by your side. So far, you embody the old adage: early to bed, early to rise, makes a man healthy, wealthy, and wise.

You generally sleep from 8:30 p.m. to 5:30 or 6:00 a.m. Even I envy you, and I am one of the all-time champion sleepers myself. When you wake early in the morning, we bring you into our bed and snuggle with you between us. Sometimes we all get another hour of sleep!

More often, you gain increasing consciousness and after fifteen minutes or so, are climbing all over our heads, crawling around the bed, playing with a few of the stuffed animals we keep nearby or with mom's curling iron, or the flashlight, giggling and laughing and making all kinds of funny sounds that tell us you are a happy, secure, intelligent little dude.

Soon it's time to get up and take Reggie for a walk and to feed you in your highchair in the kitchen. And another day has begun.

I'll save my appreciation of your appetite for another installment, which I hope will be sooner and more often forthcoming since we completed your "Baby's First Year" calendar. It was fun hanging with you today Lofton; I hope we have many more to come before our lives are finished.

May 17

Interesting, is it not: since my previous installment, you have been waking in the night, sometimes just a couple of hours after falling to sleep, every night by around 1:30 or 2:00 a.m. And we've gotten a bit lax with our policy of not picking you up out of your crib. Not surprisingly, you have figured out a means for getting back into our bed and seem just to want that, because you've been falling right back to sleep once you're between our two pillows, and sleeping through till your usual 6-am-ish wakeup.

I must admit I enjoy waking to the sounds of you giggling or squeaking near my head, and to the feeling of you crawling all over our bodies in the king-sized bed we love so. We both get a little anxious when you are near the edge because it's a good sized drop onto hardwood flooring and that's not a pretty way to start the day.

You have managed to fall off our bed a couple of times by now—maybe three—and even landed on your head the first time. Boy, that was a nasty looking bump for a while, and you cried and cried. I felt terrible, too, because it happened when your mom was at work and it was just you and me in the house. T, our neurosurgeon friend, assured me you weren't hurt badly, though, and described what tough and resilient critters are human babies; sure enough, you bounced back and were your same old self the very next day.

Still, we'd rather you not fall off the bed again, especially first thing in the morning. It's important to set a good tone for the day with your first thoughts and actions.

I can see very clearly how it works with you: if your morning is happy and mellow, the day tends to be good, emotionally even-keeled. But it also continues to apply throughout your life, and I see now the ways I'm affected by that truth. I see also how much work I have to do in order to take control of my life, even at 40 years, almost 41 years old.

In any event, I thought it was quite interesting, just as I set out what a great sleeper you've been since you were an infant, you come up with an inability to make it through the night without waking in tears, to be consoled only by the trip from your crib to our bed.

This is irony. It's something by which our lives and our culture seems sometimes defined. I wonder what role irony will play in your life and in the culture into which you mature.

And there you have it: it's 12:30 a.m.

Tonight you woke crying a little earlier than usual. I just went in to comfort you, and stayed by your side till you fell back to sleep.

Maybe tonight you'll sleep through 'till 6:00.

June 5

There are really no words to describe how incredible you seem to me. Each day you awake with a smile and giggle, bounding from one end of the bed to another, climbing on our heads, pulling at our hair, slapping at our faces as if to say, "How can you guys be sleeping when this world is here, ready to be explored!"

You are on "Go" from then, well into the late morning. Some days you are willing to take a nap near midday, anywhere from a half-hour to an hour or so. Others, you seem to run out of steam in the afternoon and will rest for an hour and a half or more. Still others, you believe there is too much to miss and you power through the day without napping at all.

Those days, the dinner hour and early evening are not especially fun for us. You are tired and cranky and likely to fall down or bang your head on something or treat us to a good forty-five minutes of crying. But the bath and bottle almost always set you right, and by somewhere between 8:00 and 9:00, you are sleeping soundly, and we have the opportunity to check ourselves, to see how we are faring.

In the last month we have begun to leave you with a caretaker for parts of a few days a week. Her name is Tita and she is from El Salvador. She is the cousin of Raina, who keeps your friend Lyla. Tita comes to Lyla's house, where we leave the four of you to play and eat and nap for four or five hours on Mondays and Fridays; sometimes on Tuesdays, too.

If you have any facility for speaking Spanish, it will be because Tita and Raina spoke it with you when you were a year old. You can't imagine how good this is for us. And for you. Your mom and I get the opportunity to practice yoga, which I hope you will adopt as a practice by the time you are seven, to use its magic and wisdom to carry you on life's winding road well into your old age.

I only discovered yoga in my thirties and am just now beginning to feel like I understand its potential for helping me find balance and satisfaction in life, which everyone—whether they admit it or not—seeks. Your mom and I also have an opportunity to spend some time alone together, freed of our anxiety over making sure you are safe and well. You get the benefit of spending time with another toddler, Lyla, with whom you apparently play very well, sharing toys and having fun in the park together, building a very sweet friendship.

I wonder if you will even know her by the time you first read this.[15]

We believe it's also a great benefit for you to spend time alone with other adults. From what we hear about your behavior when we are away from you, we are very thankful you seem to be genuinely happy and secure in your world.

Everything I have read about early childhood development points to the first three years of your life as the most crucial time for laying the emotional and behavioral foundations on which you will build your entire existence.

Feeling secure, coming to explore and experience the earth in all its beauty and power at the very beginning of your life, when you are so new to it all, gives you an opportunity later in your life, when you understand the interconnectedness of things, to harness your natural abilities to the beauty and power around you and create a wonderful existence for yourself and for those you love.

This is my goal for you. Everything I do now is designed to let you know the world as it really is—good, bad, and ugly—so that one day you may find peace in it.

June 30

Today was a Saturday. One of your mom's long work days. Right after breakfast, around 10:30, you and I left again for a trip to the East Bay. This time it was much smoother than the last one, owing, no doubt, at least in part, to our early start.

Now, A and C have a baby girl, whose name is Sonya. She was six weeks old yesterday and her folks invited us for a little walk in Tilden Park.

---

[15]   Beating the odds, you do still know Lyla and Clare, your first two "friends." It helps, I suspect, that your mom has remained friends with their parents but I think it's wonderful you have living connections to this earliest time of your life.

Tilden is a very beautiful place high in the East Bay hills where land has been preserved and maintained as a nature sanctuary and recreation area, one of the places that makes living where we do so special.

You and I already had a big day planned because your mom's new car had to go into the dealer's for service, which would entail a crossing of the Golden Gate bridge, so I figured we'd just get up a head of steam with the trip over the Bay Bridge to Berkeley, have a brisk, sunny walk in the woods, and then shoot to Marin over the Richmond Bridge for the car servicing portion of the festivities, before heading home over the Golden Gate.

It was a beautiful plan that worked beautifully.

The day was gorgeous. You were so alert and interested in all the new scenery, standing tiptoe in the pack on my back as we walked in Tilden Park, craning to follow people's dogs passing us on the trail, pointing up to birds and butterflies overhead. We talked of arranging a camping trip soon, where we'd all sleep outdoors in tents and really live, for one day, outside in nature. We also talked of other trips we could take, more adventurous and out-of-doors than a one night car-camping, with you and Sonya—and others of our friends and their children—in ten years or so. So much fun that could be, but today we had today. And today we had fun.

After the hike, you and I said good-bye to our friends and made for our second bridge crossing of the day. After we got to the Marin side, we ran into the obligatory weekend freeway snafu, but today it served a purpose in keeping us from arriving at the service appointment a half hour early.

You and I generally enjoyed the ride, listening to Lenny Kravitz while snacking on potato crisps and graham crackers for thirty minutes until the traffic found a way to disperse itself. You charmed them at the dealership and we got out of there relatively painlessly. We headed back to the City and it was still only 3:00 on a lovely day. We crossed the Golden Gate under warm clear skies in easy traffic and I decided we needed to go to the park.

We'd been with mom on Thursday this week and you loved it, playing in the grass, running into the flower beds, so I thought another visit was in order.

Today we went to "hippie hill," where lots of people congregate to dance and sing and do what they call "tribal" drumming. You were fascinated at the sights and sounds of it all and I watched you, amazed at your curiosity and your fearlessness. People smile when you come up to them because they see you smiling as you do; you are definitely a force of positivity, Lofton.

One woman was so taken with you today she began crying, your precious nature touched her so.

A short stop by the swingset and the sandbox and we were on our way home. You didn't really want to leave, but I knew it had already been a long day, we were out of food, and I didn't want you to be too tired when we got back to the house.

I ordered up some Chinese food to be delivered and you thoroughly enjoyed an entire order of tofu & broccoli; well, the tofu anyway. The broccoli your mom and I will end up eating tomorrow. After dinner you amused yourself, and me, for almost twenty minutes with two empty paper sacks and a couple of boxes of macaroni and cheese, then, after several laps around the apartment, it was time for a bath. Have I mentioned how glad I am that you seem to love the water? Oh, the fun we will have if it's really true.

You've been asleep in your crib since dozing off to a bedtime story around 9:00. It's almost 11:30 now and I'm beginning to work on my own bedtime strategy.

The ends of my days, I feel very tired at this point in my life. It's not a weary tired, though. It's a feeling that comes from knowing I put myself into something during the day; it's the kind of tired a good night's sleep can replenish. And so tomorrow, after a good night's sleep, we'll look for more adventures and new ways to get tired by tomorrow night.

SEPTEMBER 11, 2001

This date will be one of the most recognized, memorized, eulogized dates you may ever encounter. Today, unknown forces caused the destruction of the World Trade Center in the heart of the financial community on the island of Manhattan in New York, and significant damage at the nation's foremost military command post, the Pentagon, in Washington, DC.

No one knows at this point the full extent of what happened. People are simply mesmerized by the sounds and images of two iconic buildings in the broad American skyline coming completely unglued, falling down to pillars of dust and debris inside a period of two hours, on live television, and recorded on tape for people all over the world to witness.

It is difficult for me to try and write to you about these events, not only because I have difficulty assimilating the true import of what has happened today, but also, in an inescapable way, because what happened today may never be fully understood.

At best, I can give you a clear description of the way this most "earth-shattering" event of my lifetime unfolds. You may have a far better chance than I of understanding, one day, today's gravity and its effect on life in this world.

Suffice it to say—this is my belief, and one I hope many others share—we have been presented an opportunity to imagine a world where people and other beings can live in peace.[16]

It may seem odd to say that in the wake of such incredible destruction. You might think it an unnatural response to the snuffing out of thousands of lives. But always remember this, Lofton: In every pain, in every sorrow, there is a gift, which, when you can recognize it, allows you to become free of pain and to know true joy.

Today we know the utter pain and sorrow of a hatred we never thought could exist toward our country. But, in having been so awakened, we have the opportunity to examine ourselves and our place in this world, to do what we can to turn that hatred into love, that pain and sorrow into peace and happiness. Likely not in my lifetime, but perhaps in yours.

Very few people alive in the world today could honestly say they ever in their wildest fantasy imagined four commercial airline flights would be hijacked after departing nearly simultaneously from three different airports, be commandeered and (apparently) piloted by the hijackers, and used as suicide bombs against targets populated by tens

---

[16] Spoiler alert: Twenty years on, the United States will remain at war in both Afghanistan, which we will invade shortly in retribution for harboring Osama Bin Laden, one of the masterminds of the 9/11 attacks, and in Iraq, which we will invade in 2003 in a misguided belief that democracy can be imposed on people.

of thousands of innocent working people. Today's events prove the possibility of everything people have ever been unable to imagine.

The history of mankind (an astounding oxymoron) is one unfailingly characterized by sickening brutality, by senseless destruction of life, property, and the environment that sustains life. Filled too, with works of immense beauty, kindness, and grace. In a way, all of life is the manifestation of the struggle between Good and Evil. Our history as a species is the story of our inability to agree on what those terms mean.

Today, I think much of the world would agree, Evil came calling on the United States.

September 16

By now a war has been declared. More people seem sure to die. The idea of seeing last Tuesday's tragic destruction as an impetus for finding peace has not yet caught on, though I will continue to be its champion.

I am disappointed, as I have often been, in the people we have chosen to lead the nation, and the world. And I'm fearful they will exacerbate the effects of evil by their embrace of the demands of War. When will we ever learn?

No survivors have been found at any of the sites. More than 3,000 people would seem to have perished. I am so very sad.

September 17

A woman by the name of Barbara Lee, the congressional representative from Oakland, CA, was the lone member of the government's two legislative houses to cast a vote opposing Congress 'war preparations resolution last week.

She voted that way, she said, simply "because violence begets violence," and we must one day draw the line against it or it will forever plague our existence. Four hundred and twenty members of the House of Representatives voted the other way from her. I wonder if you can imagine the courage and the faith it took for her to vote in opposition to such overwhelming support for war. Barbara Lee is the kind of person I have always aspired to be, a person who sees clearly the choices before me and makes mine without regard to the leanings of the crowd I'm in.

I hope you will grow to understand and appreciate the rarity and the value of people like Barbara Lee, and make those people the crowd you are in.

October 9

Two days ago, the United States, backed by a worldwide coalition of other governments, began dropping bombs on Afghanistan. It is the first salvo in what we are calling the "War on Terrorism." It is the latest salvo in a war declared many years ago by the reputed mastermind of the September 11 attacks, Osama bin Laden, who heads a network of Islamic revolutionaries bent on the destruction of the United States and the eventual triumph of a fundamentalist brand of Islam, one of the world's oldest religions.

In a sense, then, it is a Holy War, though our leaders lack the courage and the self-awareness required to call it that.

I have yet to hear the term used in our media, but, for all practical purposes, World War III has begun.

And like all wars, this one is unholy in every respect. Read history, and see how mankind has failed to learn the lessons of life. World War I (originally called the Great War) was supposed to be the war to end all wars. World War II was supposed to be the war where Good finally triumphed over Evil. But our failure to learn goes back to the dawn of time.

Pick any epoch and read the history of how civilizations rose and how they eventually fell to the petty bickering of people who could not figure out a way to get along, could not agree to share this earthly paradise, and, almost without exception, who used the excuse of religion to justify the slaughter and destruction of their fellow man.

It has been said history is written by the winners, but I'm here to tell you we are all losers when we still justify the killing of one another under the banner of some religious mandate.

So here's the situation: There are perhaps a billion or so people all over the world who practice the faith of Islam in one form or another. Osama bin Laden purports to speak for all of them in calling for the destruction of the United States and of Israel, our close ally and the traditional foe of Muslims in the Middle East.

Our President, George W. Bush, purports to speak for us (and most of the rest of the world, another two billion or so people), in calling for the destruction of Osama bin Laden and his network of Islamic revolutionaries as the only hope we have for living in peace on this planet.

The lines have been drawn. The battle has begun. God save us all.

OCTOBER 10, 2001—SAN FRANCISCO

Here is something I wrote in response to my friend TR (who introduced me to your mom). We have been discussing these things very heatedly over the past few weeks. She is of the opinion that the terrorists cannot be dealt with as rational people and our only hope for salvation and peace lies in their destruction.

I, of course, am of the opinion that our only hope for survival, let alone peace, lies in a recognition that violence begets violence; we must stop the violence at all costs if we are to survive as a species on this planet.

To the vast multitudes who have joined this holy war, you who are steadfast in your certainty that death must immediately befall those who would threaten the lives of innocents anywhere (especially should those innocents be fortunate citizens of the greatest, most powerful, noble, and benevolent nation ever to grace the pages of human history). Here is my plea:

I do not purport to speak as a pacifist, nor as an apologist for the acts of terrorist fanatics, upon whom death must surely ascend if Civilization is to be spared the scourge of their insanity. I speak not as a congregant of any religion, nor as a citizen of any nation; not as a member of any community, nor even as the head of my own family. I speak only for myself, as one voice among the billions whose might be raised in supplication to the Power that Be, hear my plea:

Everyone must want to get on with the joy of raising their children, get on with the business of building their communities, trading their goods, creating their art, healing their sick, and celebrating their festivals and

114

holidays in peace and tranquility. Everyone would surely prefer to live lives free of feeling their very being is under attack, free of fearing their very existence on this earth could be snuffed by the violent insanity of evil creatures bent on creating a Hell of this temporal plane.

Yes, I feel sure everyone thirsts only for freedom to savor the sweet nectar of God's creation unlaced with the bitter taste of mankind's worst intentions. That would be refreshing, indeed.

It seems, however, all faiths and philosophies agree: The road to our salvation, the path to Paradise—be it here on earth or in some heavenly great beyond—is an arduous one. I thank you for your willingness to share with me the burdens you carry on your journey, just as you allow me to share mine with you. Hang in there. The hard work we do now in finding our way out of the wilderness we've sown around our hopes and dreams of heavenly glory will surely help us to one day revel in the true and infinite comfort of God's Love, the promise of our final reward.

From time immemorial—beginning with the first siblings set on this earth by our creator (as described in the Pentateuch by the story of Cain and Abel)—we human beings have been at one another's throats, desperately grasping for approval of our existence. Father, choose me upon whom to bestow your many blessings, for I, and not my brother, am the most good, the most reverent, the most loving. So fervently do I believe this, in fact, I will kill my brother as proof for you.

Over the many millennia, continually, consistently, without cease, great armies have been raised. Vast fields of human aspiration have been flooded and laid waste in the service of mankind's insatiable need to be validated, and to be forgiven the taste for our own blood. From the very beginning it has always been thus; why should the plot line of our existence on this earth change now? Surely we are destined to know the peace for which all good men strive once the last bad man is hunted down, flushed out, and killed in sacrifice on the altar of our Love for God.

How could I have been so blind to not see this?

But I confess: I do not have the strength, nor the courage, to wield the sword of such human kindness. Should I be cut down myself one day, as surely as Abel was slain by his own brother, I must accept that fate. Because I am weak and afraid to look upon any man to smite him in the name of God, I must entrust my fate to those, like you, who, with the clear vision of what is good and who is evil, have the courage and the will to do the awful, thankless, heartrending—but necessary—work of ridding God's creation of all that is not good, of cleansing it of all who are unholy in the eyes of the Father.

Have mercy.

Now, you may well vilify me as holier-than-thou, asking, "What is your solution to the problems vexing our world in this terrible time?" And again I would confess: I have no answer.

You are certain of your answer, however. I will thus bear witness, in humble awe of your steadfast belief in the rightness of your actions, to all that shall be wrought in the wake of your fury, to all left standing among the debris of your terrible justice.

May God look upon your works and be pleased.

OCTOBER 16

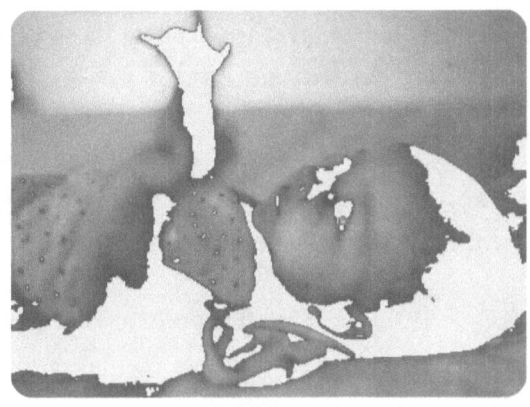

But enough of the weight of the world. To dwell upon the past or live for some future reward misses the point entirely.

Life occurs in each and every moment, every one so precious in its fleeting nature. You may one day be overwhelmed by the depth and treasure of all the moments that came before the one in which you live right now. The histories, oral and written, recorded and filmed, preserved for your benefit, presented for your education and entertainment; revel in them, study them, question and examine them all; know where you come from.

You may have a great capacity for imagining fantastical futurities, a visionary understanding of the directions and possibilities for your generation of humankind. And you may work tirelessly, heroically, to see them come to pass. Some future history may sing praises of you. But the moment in which you live and breathe, right now, is the most precious there will ever be; for there will never be another like it.

I've understood this myself a brief while, perhaps ten or fifteen of my forty-one years. And I've managed to truly live in the moment a handful of times in that span.

Of course, I continue working diligently toward increasing my ratio of appreciated moments to lived ones, and I point all this out only in the hope you may get started earlier than I did.

Funny actually, these days, your very presence is a lesson in this philosophy. For, as an eighteen-month-old child, you have no capacity for living in anything other than the moment!

You are beginning to exhibit signs of memory. You recognize people you have seen before; you can recall where you left your shoe or your cup, or something dear to you, twenty minutes ago, or even yesterday. You recognize all the places in our home now; you even seem to be familiar with some of the places we go on our daily errands, like to the bank or the grocery, the post office, to Nickie's, and to your friend Lyla's house.

So your concepts of time and space are beginning to broaden. But you live in the moment, dude. You are happy when you are happy, and you are upset when you are upset. And the space between the two extremes can be as the blink of an eye. It's a challenge for me and your mom because, as adults, we have been conditioned away from living in the moment for so long (as life will condition you, too, as you grow older).

Your demand that we do so (live in the moment) now can be a little disorienting. Speaking for myself, I love it. But then, I've always enjoyed disorientation to a large degree, a legacy, perhaps, of my understanding of the principle of ecstasy. How do I know where I stand if I cannot get outside of myself to see?

In a couple of days (permitting myself now the luxury of living in the future), we will go to Hawaii for a yoga retreat. Hawaii is America's Paradise. Eight islands in the middle of the Pacific Ocean where the spirit of the earth and the power of freedom find a synergy like nowhere else. Once there, we'll have nine days to revitalize our energies, leaving aside the travails of the political world, to bask in chances for living in the moment as part of the crowd we'll be practicing yoga with. You will have great fun, I am sure, traipsing around the volcanoes and swimming in the placid waters of the great Pacific Ocean, and I hope this early exposure to the unique forces prevailing in Hawaii will gird you in a need for awareness as your life becomes more complicated.

I hope for soft breezes and warm nights to bless the love I have for you and for your mom, for our family, to give us the strength and the nourishment we need to persevere in this mean old world.

NOVEMBER 25

Today was a milestone day.

I may have referred previously to your early talent for throwing a ball. If not, I've been remiss, because, since you were about six months old you have had what I call a great arm.

It's been such fun for me throwing balls with you these last several months. But today, you learned to catch. Not just one lucky catch either, where the right-sized ball lands in the right spot between your arms and your chest. No, today you made several honest catches, where you watched the ball into your hands and saw for the first time the possibilities of throwing and catching together.

We are starting to have fun.

You love watching people play frisbee in the park, and you'll throw or kick just about any kind of ball for several minutes at a stretch, squeaking and giggling at the fun of it all. This past summer, you were a big baseball fan (baseball was one of your first ten words). We went to some Giants games, and watched lots of other games together on TV all the way through the World Series. For a while there, you couldn't walk past the cabinet where we keep the television in the living room without pointing up to it and saying, "baseball."

I kid you not.

Now, the football season is in full swing, cresting the midseason rise toward a denouement of year-end college bowl games and the professional playoffs. To the great joy of your mother, because it is a dangerous sport, you haven't shown too much interest in football, so far.

I always thought I'd try and spare you the effects of TV longer than we've apparently managed. I guess for just about your whole first year you didn't get exposed to much of it. But these past nine months have seen a steady increase in your TV viewing. I feel you are probably OK with it because you invariably abandon the set when commercials appear. For that matter, you often find a lot of what passes for "children's programming" uninteresting, and you'll walk away from the TV for a book or a ball-toss or a little wrestling around with ease.

Even more remarkably, according to child development research, your ability to sit and focus for fifteen and twenty minutes at a time on a program you find interesting is quite unusual for your age group. You're only a year-and-a-half old, and you're watching TV at a four-year-old level. (That's supposed to be a joke.)

All and all, you seem to prefer the great outdoors, which makes me happy. I can only hope the winds of fate will breathe many more years of life into my desire to share my own love for the outdoors with you. In the coming months, the snows of Lake Tahoe will beckon, and who knows, perhaps you'll have a White Christmas in Memphis in a few weeks.

There I go, drifting from the moment again. As I was saying...today was a milestone day.

A SIDE NOTE ON FOOTBALL SUNDAYS, JUSTICE, AND WHERE YOU SPEND YOUR PERSONAL ENERGY

In 2012 the NFL would lock its referees out during the pre-season, amidst a labor dispute over the referees' demands for higher pay and benefits. The league and the referees' union were arguing about what amounted to $3.2 million in increased costs for the league, roughly four hundredths of a percent of the $9 billion in revenue generated annually by the league.

The league brought in replacement referees, otherwise known as "scabs" in the parlance of labor disputes, which turned out to be a complete disaster as they lacked the experience to adjust to the speed of the game played at the NFL level and were incapable of enforcing the various players' safety rules. Everyone thought, "Surely they will settle this thing before the official start of the season."

But no, there we were on the first Monday night of the regular season with referees from the Lingerie Football League (a short-lived entertainment spectacle in which women wearing helmets and shoulder pads played football in uniforms comprised of bras and panties), completely fucking up a game between my beloved Packers and the Seattle Seahawks.

Lofton and I would be there, watching the game on TV over at D's house, along with three or four of my closest friends. At the end of a back-and-forth battle, the Packers would be up by 5 points, with the Seahawks needing a touchdown to win the game as time was running out. A last-second Hail Mary pass from the Seahawks' QB was grabbed at the back of the end zone simultaneously by a Seahawks receiver and a Packers defensive back, and as the two players fell to the ground, the Packers player clearly came away with possession of the ball.

Interception in the end zone, Packers win.

But no. The referees called it a touchdown for the Seahawks; six points, Seahawks win.

I couldn't believe it. Neither could the Packers' coach, who threw his challenge flag, and so the referees assembled on the sidelines to review the play.

During the TV break, while the review was underway, I announced to the room, "If they don't reverse this call, I will never watch another NFL football game for the rest of my life."

My friends would howl with laughter, believing they'd heard yet another hyperbolic pronouncement from the lips of a guy who'd been known to exaggerate from time to time. The broadcast resumed and the head referee announced, "After further review, the call on the field stands; touchdown Seahawks."

And that was that.

Eight years later, I have yet to watch a full NFL game again. Because the league and the games are such an inescapable part of the culture between September and February, I have not managed to completely avoid them, but that experience in 2012 would forever change my view of professional sports—especially of the NFL itself—and, happily, create space in my consciousness and in my schedule, for so many things that would ordinarily take a backseat to my bandwidth for football.

Since then, my Sundays (Monday nights and Thursdays, now, too) in fall and wintertime have been free of the anticipation and anxiety that can build before a Packers game. I'm able to spend that time riding Bay Area backroads on my bicycle, which is surely far better for my health than spending hours with my stomach in knots, filling it with salty snacks and alcohol.

I've been able to cultivate a regime and routine my girlfriend and I call "Self-care Sundays," which involves yoga and meditation, slowing down and getting centered for the week to come, which seems a wiser use of precious time than participating in a competition ritual dedicated to making more money for people who have quite enough of it already.

DECEMBER 16

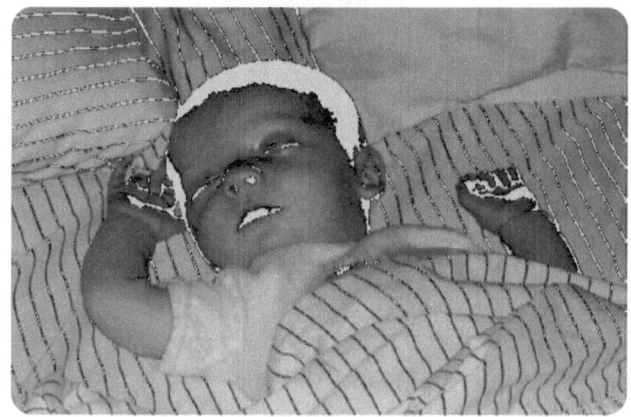

Y ou are sleeping now, taking your midday nap in your room, snuggled comfortably in your stroller, strains of music from Malawi playing softly on your dresser top. I hope you'll rest for at least an hour so I can make a journal entry here and listen to the Green Bay Packers' game on internet radio.

It's a cold, bright Sunday afternoon outside and my guess is your mom will take you to the playground when you wake, where you will run around, climb on the jungle-gym, and kick and throw whatever balls may be found up there.

Speaking of sleep, your nighttime sleeping has become very regular and effortless for all of us. You know when it's bedtime now, and when you are tired enough from a full day of playing and exploring, you may even ask to go "night-night." You average nine-to-ten hours of pretty uninterrupted sleep, sometimes waking briefly to let out a whine or a few yelps, but then you lie back down on your pillow and return to sleep. When you wake up early in the morning, we bring you to our bed and the three of us languish among the pillows and fluffy covers; occasionally we all get a little more slumber, but more often within a half-hour you are climbing down from the bed and saying "bye-bye" or "see you," and our day begins.

You spend large amounts of every day naming all the things you see and come across. I love it when you come running to me with eyes wide and excitement in your voice, saying "Zebra, zebra, zebra," holding aloft a little zebra from your alphabet zoo. (PACKERS TOUCHDOWN!) You can't eat a meal without making sure everyone knows you are using your "spoon," your "cup," and your "plate." You must hold up your food and announce "peas," or "bagel," or "fajita" before you commence to putting in as much as your mouth will hold. You are full of curiosity and fearlessness, and you approach almost all people with a smile on your face and kindness in your manner.

Sometimes I feel my heart will burst trying to hold the love I feel for you.

By now you have close to a hundred words in your English vocabulary and a half-dozen or so, maybe more, in Spanish. And it seems like you are gaining one or two every day. You are also beginning to show you understand relationships between things.

You don't simply understand that a light is "light," but you understand it helps you to "see" in dark places if it is a flashlight, and that it is "hot" if it is coming from a bulb you can touch.

You know you can come to your mother with arms outstretched, saying "Up! up!" and she will take you in her arms and smother you with hugs and kisses; you also know when we are riding in the car and we encounter one of San Francisco's famous hills we go "up" or "down."

This understanding is all very impressive to me. I truly honor and respect you as a magnificent creature.

Another of your characteristics I find fascinating is your interest in music and rhythm. Last night we went to a surprise birthday party for Lyla's dad, AM. There were several other kids, Rose, Georgia, and Clare among them, and you all played well together with the toys and balls and playhouse tunnels downstairs at our hosts' house. You ate pizza and tofu and drank apple juice and I think y'all had at least as much fun as we adults did upstairs.

For our entertainment Lyla's mom hired a couple of guys to sit in the living room and play guitar. Toward the end of the night, when there were only a few guests remaining, you and Lyla and Rose came upstairs, where six or eight of us were milling around, enjoying the guitar duo performing their last couple of songs. First you went right up to them and danced with a big smile on your face. Then you sat down and watched intently as one of them played most of a fugue by Bach. Your attention was rapt and I couldn't believe you were able to so focus on the music with all the other distractions in the room.

Then the truly amazing part happened. As the boys rose to put their instruments away and call it a night, you made it very clear that no one was going anywhere until you had an opportunity to play.

One of the guitarists sat down and held the guitar for you and you played a very spare, very composed melody, helped, of course, by the knowing hands of the guitarist controlling the fretboard. But there you stood, for several minutes, exploring the strings and the resonance of the guitar body, not flailing wildly as some toddlers might, but playing each string carefully, fully aware you were making music.

Or so it seemed to me.

All the other adults standing around with their mouths agape agreed it was a fairly remarkable performance and we all clapped for you when you were finished. Should you grow to be a musician, you may fairly and honestly say your first public performance came before you were yet two years old.

Well, the Packers are having a little trouble down in Tennessee here at the end of the first half, so I'm going in search of a sports bar to try rooting them home to victory. And, as the subtle synchronicities of life's ever-changing energies would have it, you just woke up—it's been a little over an hour nap for you.

Your mom has you in her arms now, standing in the kitchen with you nuzzling the side of her neck. Soon you'll be running around the playground, finding some new way to amaze us all with your magnificence.

DECEMBER 30

It occurs to me this writing appears headed toward unabashed, enthusiastic celebration of your developing presence in life, and I might temper my portrayal of you as a child of unique and boundless gifts if I'm to serve you well in finding a balanced understanding of things.

You see, all people are magnificent creations. No one of the many billions of us who scurry about this earth is any more magnificent than any other. Each of us has but one basic desire: to be happy.

Many of life's difficulties arise from the wildly different ideas people have for becoming happy, and from varying resources and abilities in putting them into practice. So when I go on about how smart, or observant, or talented, or skillful you are, you should understand there are countless others just like you living at the moment you read this, who lived before you into the infinite past, who will come after you into the limitless future. When you can recognize that truth about everyone you meet, when you can see your own life and your own experience in them and in their lives, you will begin to find your way in the world and understand the true nature of your own gifts.

Having said that, at this point in your life, you are universally regarded as adorable and your presence is a light wherever you go. People look upon you and smile. Some are drawn to you and seem compelled to remark on your many virtues.

You carry yourself with a light, gentle ease, full of humor, rhythm, and inquisitiveness, and though you have your frustrations in coming to terms with your own independence (and therefore, with the fact of everyone's independence: no, you can't always get what you want), you are the greatest.

2002

January 29

A new year is upon us. A month gone by since I wrote to you last. Time moves very rapidly for me now, though I can still remember the feelings I had as a child—anguished and impatient at time's lack of progress.

Time is no constant, though we do our best to mark and quantify it. It's a neat trick, savoring each moment's unique, ephemeral preciousness, and understanding the present's relation to what has passed before and to what may lie ahead. If you can live as though each moment may be your last while understanding you have all the time in the world, you might get close to the true nature of time.

Little has changed since the turn of the year. Your mom's leave from her employment is coming to an end soon, and that bodes some rearrangement in our routine. I'm contemplating a road-trip for you and I down to Los Angeles toward the beginning of March. I ran it by your mom, and her initial reaction was positive, so we'll see. She'll have to be back at work by the end of that month, so I think she'll appreciate a little time alone and some space to herself before she leaves behind the cozy little home life we've enjoyed together since last August.

We've been getting you outside quite a bit more in recent weeks. Generally to the schoolyard across the street and to a nearby playground, where you have begun to find yourself very much at home. We've even joined a Tiny Tots program at the playground on Tuesdays, where you participate with several other kids in some semi-organized activities like ball games and art sessions. You seem to enjoy it and have done well with the other children.

Today you impressed me with your memory. As we were dressing to go run some errands after lunch, I realized your regular shoes were wet and dirty from earlier in the day. So I went to your closet and you picked out your red sneakers, which you hadn't worn in at least a month.

I was putting them on you when you pointed to them, looked at me and said, "party." I understood you to remember we refer to those red sneakers as your "party shoes" because they got some very good wear this past holiday season at the several holiday parties we went to.

Your vocabulary is shaping up and you are beginning to show a mastery of complex relationships between people, objects, and now, time.

I continue to be awed at the miracle of life as I see it through your growth.

In the words of the comedian Dana Carvey, "I am weakened by the power of your cuteness."

February 9

This has been a watershed week. On Monday we received an offer from a couple of guys wanting to buy our house. Your Mom and I have lived here nearly ten years—almost the entire time she has spent in San Francisco. We rented our apartment for eight years, then bought it, along with the unit below us, two years ago with the help of my friend and business partner, D. He's a successful real estate agent in his working life and he, for one reason or another, decided last fall he wanted to pull his investment out of our property here.

He and I made our assessment of the market and priced the building at what we believed to be the high end of fair value. We showed it often, though to very few prospective buyers, during the fall and into the year-end holiday season, and got no offers at all.

None of us was too surprised, given we'd priced it rather dearly and the year-end isn't exactly a robust period for real estate transactions.

But the new year brought out some buyers and in just a few weeks, many people came through the place—and we got an offer that exceeded our expectations. So now we will move to a new place. All of the things we are accustomed to, the places familiar to us, the paths and stations of our everyday lives, our rooms and views, the sounds and smells of our days and nights, will change.

I can't remember if it was William Blake who said, "Without change there is no progression," but I know my experience of life has proven it true to me. So I'm excited about the prospects of finding a new place to call home.

I think your mom would probably prefer to stay where we are—she has a very strong instinct to settle, to root, to cultivate, and grow. Her farmers' genes. One of the reasons I married her, I suspect.

I, on the other hand, have a hard time sitting still for too long. I love to roam and explore and encounter all the varied places and peoples of this world. Home to me, in some ways, is wherever I may be. It's how I'd like it to be, anyway.

So, we'll move.

I hope we can find a place with better weather and a little deck or yard space outside for you to run around in. The house we move into now will probably be the first house you remember growing up in, so I want to be sure it's a place where you'll feel safe and free.

February 26

The search for new digs continues. Sadly, we've thus far found nothing to meet our needs or expectations. It's been very, very stressful, not only because we no longer have a choice about it, not only because your mom has to return to work in only three weeks, and not only because we're a little particular about the kind of place we're looking for, but mostly because people here are, to put it kindly, unrealistic about the value of housing.

Now, San Francisco is roundly considered one of the premier cities of the entire world, much of which has to do with the stunning beauty and variety of the natural landscape surrounding it. Its culture is also as rich and diverse as you'll find in any city in America, certainly. And there are some truly magnificent homes here that would command top dollar no matter where they might be located.

We are faced with a situation, though, in which, up until quite recently, the economy has been over-inflated by rapid growth in technology, which led to high salaries being paid to people with skills in technological fields, many of whom moved to San Francisco—the epicenter of the technology industry.

It's a small place, with a limited number of housing units, and the simple laws of supply and demand dictated a massive spike over the past six months in the prices people are willing to pay for housing.

But then the growth boom went bust.

Companies shut down, a lot of people lost their jobs. They had to leave the houses they were paying outrageous amounts to rent, but many property owners have yet to return to the reality of what average working people can afford to pay for a place to live in.

While the natural ebb-and-flow of life brings vacancies onto the housing market, property owners who may have missed out on the high rents their fellow owners were enjoying until recently, now are pricing their newly vacant places at prices much higher than they might ask in a "normal" market.

You wouldn't believe some of the absolute dumps we have looked at for prices nearly three times the rent we paid when we moved here ten years ago.

But, we remain optimistic, your mom and I. We know we'll find the right spot at the right price for us. We may succumb to the stresses involved in doing so and we may argue more than usual, and I worry about the ways our frustrations and short-temperedness might be affecting you.

This is a very, very impressionable time in your life and you are soaking up every detail of the world around you, so I feel bad to be contributing elements of fear and anger and intolerance in your experience; you'll get plenty of that from many other sources as you grow older.

Meanwhile, you are doing just great. You seem very observant, very curious about your environment, very unafraid to find yourself in new places or among new people. We recently joined a music group where you get together with six or eight other kids to sing songs and play instruments and you have taken to it quite naturally. You can't imagine the joy this brings me.

You are also beginning to comprehend your independence in the world, though still from a very self-centered place: to you, everything here is here for you. Which, ironically, is the truth!

Because you don't have an understanding[17] that everything here is here for everyone else as well, and you have yet to develop a sense of compassion, nor skills in sharing and conserving the things you find around you, it's a time full of frustration for your playmates, for you, and for us—as you try to keep all the toys for yourself, or destroy things exploring your curiosity about them, or abandon other things when something new comes into your awareness.

All of this is quite normal and natural and in my view, Lofton, you are a magnificent creature to behold. Even in tempestuous moments of

---

[17] At not even two years old and as a single child to boot, you could not be expected to understand the concepts I refer to. You would go on, though, in about a year-and-a-half, to attend a wonderful, parent-participation co-op preschool, where you would spend two-and-a-half years coming to learn what it means to be an independent person of free will living in a diverse community. You would begin cultivating a strong sense of justice and fairness and, importantly in my view, an empathy and compassion for those around you who are disabled or disadvantaged. These traits would continue to develop in you and become more refined with experience and the years, along with your reasoning skills and a facility for articulating and arguing your perspective. So much so that by the time you reach your twenties, I will be regularly suggesting that you could find satisfaction and success in becoming a lawyer.

immaturity you possess a profound sweetness and a gentle nature that fills my heart with love and gladness for your presence.

So, now it's getting late and I must get to sleep (you are sleeping quite well these days, by the way: 8:30 p.m. to 6:00 a.m. straight through) so I can rise early tomorrow morning for my teaching assignment in the East Bay—a story for another time. That, and a redoubling of effort to find the perfect house for our next phase of living together....

THE BRIDGE: BOOMERS, A MILLENNIAL, AND THE FAMILY BED

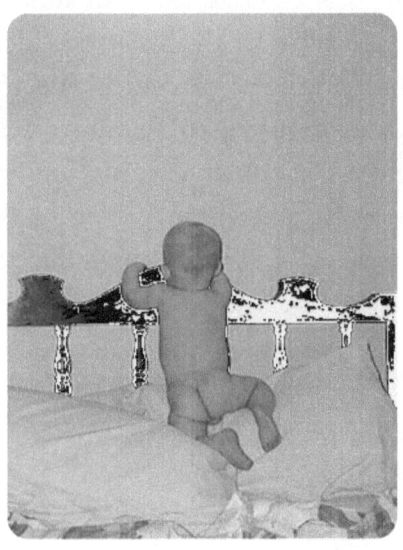

I remember a hot topic at the weekly parents' education classes your mom and I attended when you, Lofton, were in pre-school.

Not long before you turned three, we joined a co-op, where twenty families worked together with two certified early-childhood education professionals, trying to arrive at our best understanding of how children develop and what we might do to set our kids on the path to life's best opportunities.

Part of the commitment required to join the co-op included serving at the school one day a week, to help watch over the children as they went about their "work," which, as you grokked early on (and continued to remind me even five years later) is "to play." Once a month, each family also had to provide a healthy snack for all the children and adults at the school on a day different from their regular at-school work day. These work and feeding commitments may not seem much on the surface, but in a town where the single-income family is an endangered species, we all found it challenging to meet them from time to time.

What may have been the most difficult—for us adults, anyway—was the weekly meeting/education class, where we took care of the business of running the school and, with the assistance of the two educators, delved deeply into the many intricacies of child development and family health. The co-op is committed to diversity, which meant twenty families who brought a sometimes ungainly spectrum of influences, beliefs, experiences and expectations to the community. For three years, Tuesday nights were a guaranteed leap into the deep end of the emotional pool.

One of the things that came up early on and something people seemed to have definite opinions about, was the concept of "the Family Bed."

How OK is it to have children sleeping with their parents and for how long?

When is the right time and what is the best way to get children used to sleeping in their own beds?

Crying, sickness, bedwetting, bad dreams, lack of parental sleep, lack of parental privacy, control issues, punishment, reward—we went mano-a-mano with a panoply of strategies and ideas, on which everyone seemed to have a different opinion and to which there seemed no right answer.

As with many things in life that rile people up, I sought guidance from my heart on the matter of you sleeping with us and resolved for myself to pay attention to the signals you gave at bedtime to determine what would be best for you, and for us. It was easy when you were little, except in those first weeks of life, when I was sure your mom or I would roll on top of you in the middle of the night and unknowingly suffocate our little bean.

We moved you to a crib in your own room at about four or five months, if my recollection is correct, and some of my favorite times were spent sitting on the floor by the crib singing you softly to sleep. Your mom and I enjoyed the opportunity to reconnect as a couple, too, during this period, for a half year or so, until you learned to climb out of the crib and make your way back into our bed during the middle of the night.

All through pre-school, you mostly ended up in our bed, though there were times when you had a particularly exhausting day physically and slept through the night in your own room.

The summer before you started kindergarten, we got you a big-boy bed, and virtually every night, except when one or the other of us might be out of town, your mom or I would read with you and you'd fall asleep in your room. Sometimes you slept the night through, sometimes you ended up with us. It didn't ever seem to bother or matter to me and luckily, your mom felt the same way. I guess if one or the other of us had felt differently it would have caused a problem, and I'm glad we never had to confront it.

As you got older, you slept more nights through in a row and by 2nd grade you were even starting to willingly go to bed without one of us lying down to read with you first. At that age you still awoke in the middle of the night and crawled into bed with us on occasion, though. And once you got bigger, even though we slept in a king-sized bed, I was no longer under any illusion that I might accidentally smother you.

Sometimes, when I would wake in the middle of the night and notice you there asleep, or when I'd rise early in the morning to slip out of bed and start my day, I relished the incomparable joy of listening to you breathing deeply, content and secure, and at rest.

March 26

Today your mom returned to work full-time, which means you and I will be spending more time together.

You have had the kind of early experience few are afforded in this life: nearly uninterrupted contact with both of your parents, which is thought to be most important in your first three years—especially having uninterrupted contact with your mom—which you have had since she has been able to keep her job without working so much these last two years.

Some believe many problems in society stem from disadvantaged early childhood experience, which keeps people from becoming properly functioning adults. I must say from observing you and the way you behave in your world, the theories appear to have some substance behind them, problem-free as our experience has largely been.

But now your mom will be working five days a week, spending over forty hours away from home. She will only be able to spend time with you when she comes home in the evenings and on her days off. She is very sad about this because she has enjoyed being so close to you, spending so much time with you; she feels she could be missing out on some of your most important growth and development. I hope, because you and I will be together a lot, the impact of your mom's absence will be lessened and the two of you will be able to benefit greatly from whatever time you will have together until the next big change occurs in our lives.

Big changes are afoot at this moment, in any event. We found a house. One almost perfectly suited to our needs. The process of moving has begun.

Perhaps one day you will come across some discussion of the human life cycle and its rites of passage, its significant "moments," and of the means and methods by which we approach and understand them, of how we see them through. The discussion will invariably note the stress and trauma and anxiety associated with moving. We are beginning to experience the onset of those energies, but I am hopeful the lengthy period of time we will take to do the move, almost an entire month, may attenuate the extremes to which they can spike in more frantic circumstances.

You will have a great bedroom to yourself—with the best view in the house. There is also a nice outdoor space for you to play in. We are excited and anxiously looking to the next phase of our lives together.

Yesterday you and I returned from our first trip away from your mom. Last Thursday we flew to Miami, Florida, to spend time with relatives. You met my cousin, her husband, and their kids; my favorite Uncle; and a whole host of the large clan from your grandfather Buddy's side of the family. They have lived in the Miami area for many, many years.

From the time I was your age until I was nearly 24, we spent part of every year in Florida. I grew up loving the lifestyle our Florida family had. It was open and stimulating, frenetic, explorative, alive. Not that my own family's lifestyle growing up was particularly restrictive or sheltered—I just always enjoyed being among them. Plus, Florida is its own unique place in America, hanging out there on the isthmus between the Atlantic, the Caribbean, and the Gulf of Mexico. I hope you'll get to go check it out for yourself as an adult before climate change brings its irrevocable transformations.

After Buddy died, my contact with them waned, and until last week, I hadn't seen any of them since your Mom's and my wedding, nearly eleven years ago. But as in all great relationships, our reunion felt almost as though no time had passed at all. In truth, it had. The children I had known from our last encounter were now teenagers and young adults. My cousin's eight-year-old daughter, I had never met. My generation of cousins was now middle-aged; my Uncle and his wife, the elders of the clan.

Before we left, your mom was very worried about letting you go alone with me on such a long trip. I believe she had nightmares about me somehow losing you at one of the airports. But we did fine. For an under-two-year-old, you handled the unfamiliar environment, the cramped quarters, and the noise and discomfort of plane travel very well.

I took some of your favorite small toys along: a set of wooden cars and people; a few matchbox tractors, cranes, and bulldozers; a handy-dandy-notebook drawing tool. I also had a couple of DVDs to play on my computer to keep you amused, and in case things got completely out of hand, a bottle of infant antihistamine to help you remain calm and docile.

I'm proud to say we used all the toys and books and we watched both the DVDs, but I did not have to resort to drugging you. I came very close on the first leg of our return, on the flight from Miami to Minneapolis, when you spilled orange juice all over yourself and your seat in the first few minutes; but we both persevered and the trip on the whole was a great success.

At the party which was our ostensible reason for going, a fiftieth birthday celebration for one of the cousins in my generation, you met a three-year-old boy. The two of you became fast friends, and you danced and sang and played, running and jumping and howling with glee the whole time we were there. All the adults marveled at how cute and talented and energetic the two of you were. When we finally said goodnight and went upstairs to our hotel room at 11:30 p.m,. you took a quick bath and fell asleep almost immediately.

I had such fun traveling and partying with you, Lofton. I hope we have many places to go and many parties to attend before this lifetime has us part.

1986: DETAINED IN CHINA

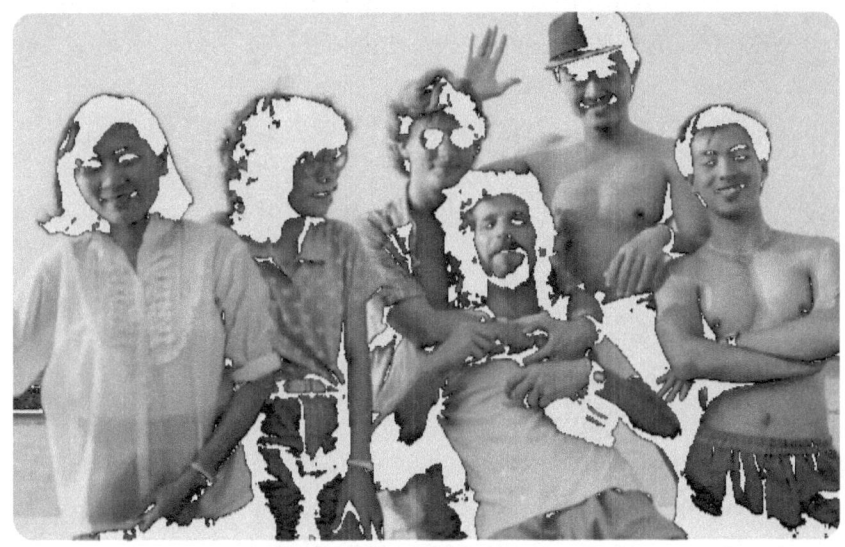

OPEN SALON EDITOR'S PICK

In the fall of 1986, I traveled to mainland China for the first time, with my friend H, a classmate from law school who shared my love of adventure and a predilection for exploring altered states in all their terrifying, magnificent glory.

I was just coming off a nine-month stint living in Taipei, Taiwan, where I'd been teaching English, learning to speak and read Mandarin, and enhancing a deep affection for the history and culture of the Chinese people. H left a successful business venture he'd launched several months prior in New Zealand, to join me on what was planned—at the time—to be a four-month tour of a vast country that was, in 1986, still largely unknown and fraught with mystery and superstition in the Western mind. He knew next-to-nothing about China. But he liked Chinese food and he loved the idea of traveling with me, so we were off.

Four months might seem like a long time, but China is large and I had learned about many places beyond the obvious big-city stops I wanted to experience and explore, and in our previous years traveling throughout Europe and Asia, H and I both gained a great appreciation for moving off the beaten path, for understanding that the most beautiful, valuable gems can be found in places where others fear, or forget to look.

This meant that I had taken great pains to study China's geography and transportation systems and to map out a route that made efficient use of time in covering the several thousand miles of territory we planned to cover in those months.

One day, in a small village west of Guilin, we sought to board a train bound for Guiyang. The train station in this small village was packed with hundreds of people coming and going—the bustle inherent around trains in China was very impressive, even in out of the way places, and as I stepped to the window to buy our tickets, several dozen people waited in line behind me. H and I were the only two white people in the place. The ticket vendor said *mei-yo*, which roughly translates to "I have none," when I presented the money for our fare, and I was confused.

I asked him again and repeated the name of our destination, thinking perhaps my pronunciation had been incorrect. Again he said, *mei-yo*. I started to get pissed. No people I have met can take the dark out of the nighttime or paint the daytime black like the Chinese. I pointed to the sign on the wall behind him with the train number and the destination clearly marked on it. I read off the other other destinations to make it clear to him that I knew what I was reading. I pointed to the train sitting on the platform outside and told him I wanted two tickets, please!

People in the line behind me grew restless. Grumbling and shouting began to build. A helpful young man stepped up to the window and asked me in Chinese what was the problem and could he help me?

I told him, "My friend and I want to go to Guiyang and this guy won't sell me the tickets. He's telling me he has none and I can see the train sitting right there and it's on the schedule right behind him and I know there are seats available on that train!"

The young man stuck his head in the window and had a pleasant, exceedingly rapid exchange with the vendor, afterward withdrawing to inform me that the vendor could not sell me the tickets. It was against the law for us to ride that train and he would lose his job if he sold us the tickets. There was nothing he could do.

Now the shouting behind us was getting louder. Pushing and shoving commenced and we were literally swept from the front of the ticket window by a wave of people who had trains to catch.

Just then three uniformed officers approached us, thanked the guy who had tried to assist us and gently, but firmly made it clear that H and I were to come with them.

Now.

We walked the hundred yards or so to the police station with the officers remaining silent in the face of my, what must have seemed to them, comical expressions of indignation rendered in barely passable Mandarin:

"What is happening? This is a mistake! We just want to go to Guiyang! I saw the train on the schedule!"

"Is this because we are foreigners?"

"This is wrong!"

"This is very bad!"

As we approached the doorway, one of the officers turned to me and said, simply, "The Captain would like a word with you. He will explain."

We were ushered into a clean, sparsely furnished office that could have served as a perfect set piece for a 1950s detective story. There was a small desk, several large filing cabinets, the obligatory portrait of Mao hanging on the wall and a small couch with two comfortable wooden chairs surrounding a low table set for tea. The captain smiled and offered us each some tea as he gestured toward the chairs and asked, in perfect English, "Where are you gentlemen headed?"

I explained to him where we wanted to go and after more conversation in which he asked us, calmly, pleasantly, how long we'd been in China, how we were enjoying our stay, where else we planned to visit and such, he said, "Guiyang is a lovely place. You will enjoy it much I think. But you cannot get there from here. The train to Guiyang is only for locals. No international travelers are permitted to ride that line. You will have to go back to Guilin and take the train from there."

He smiled and asked if there was anything else he could help us with. There was nothing to do at that point but thank the Captain for his hospitality, assure him we understood the situation and figure out how we were going to make up for the lost day of travel backtracking to Guilin was going to cost us. After all, at that point we only had three months left on our schedule.

May 11

We are finally in what you call "New House."

One of the things I love about you is your adaptability to all environments. You tend to be reserved at first when you encounter new people and new places, but invariably it isn't long before you seem as if you'd been there or known them all your life.

We moved to our home on Harper about three weeks ago. For your mom and me, it was very stressful. We'd been living on Corbett for over ten years, and we had so much stuff, so much furniture, so many tchotchkes, boxes, and boxes of things we had stored in the basement there for ten years, endless numbers of things we certainly don't need but which, for whatever reason, we never managed to give away or sell or leave behind. Packing it all up and moving it to this new location and then unpacking it and finding a place for it in the new house has been quite a job.

But we are finally here, and things are starting to feel cozy and homey, and I believe we are going to find it very agreeable.

The neighborhood is quite wonderful.

It's nice now to be able to put you in a stroller and walk a few blocks to the fruit and vegetable store, or the butcher, or the wine store, do some shopping, and come home. No getting in the car and fighting traffic and burning fuel and dealing with trying to find parking; just strolling past the playground, passing our neighbors sitting on their stoops and porches, feeling like everything has slowed down and gotten a little more settled.

And the weather here is so much better, too. We had great views from our apartment on Corbett, but it was always super windy and often quite foggy up there. One July Evening while walking our dog, Reggie, wearing a winter parka, as one does in the summer in San Francisco, I wrote "Up by My Place".[18]

---

[18]   Man, you ought to feel the wind blow up by my place
       Man, you ought to feel it blow
       Man, you ought to feel the wind blow up by my place
       Feel it blow, feel it blow
       It's got a pretty nice view
       It ain't too far out of the way
       But that wind keeps whipping through

Now, the morning sunshine streams onto our front porch and in the front windows, and we can go sit on the stoop to bask in warm light as early as seven o'clock. In the afternoon, the sun starts playing on all the trees and plants in the backyard by midday and lingers on the back deck well past 6:00 in the evening.

These days you are very talkative. I'm impressed by your memory and your cognitive abilities: you are able to make very astute and complex associations and you seem able to order your experiences in a very logical manner. I guess that's just another way of saying you seem very smart.

Take one example from yesterday.

I was picking you up from a friend's house and when I got there, her grandfather was there visiting. When I arrived, you immediately said, "Three daddies!" Your friend's dad, who you already knew; his dad (the

Every single day
Man, you ought to feel the wind blow up by my place
It comes over the hill and in through the window
Takes a smile right off your face
Man, you ought to feel it blow
Any time of the season
Any phase of the moon
Without no rhyme or reason
Morning, night, and noon
Don't matter what I do
Don't care about what I say
That wind keeps whipping through
And I keep getting blown away
Man, you ought to feel the wind blow up by my place
Man, you ought to feel it blow
It comes over the hill and in through the window
Takes a smile right off your face
I said, man, you ought to feel it blow

© 1999 L. Lazar (ASCAP) From the album SAVE YOURSELF

grandfather), who you'd just met; and me, your dad. Maybe I'm just the proud poppa, but I thought it was pretty impressive for you to not only conceive of the number three, but to also make the intergenerational connection between your friend's dad and your friend's dad's dad, and and put them both in the same "daddy box."

Life is good, Lofton, and you continue to impress upon me the precious beauty that lives in each of us. So far you are untainted, uncynical, unscarred by the stupidity and brutal impersonality of our social constructs. You are open and joyful, and playful, and strong, and I love spending time with you. You are secure and independent and I feel I can take you anywhere. Even at two, you do me proud and endear yourself to everyone you meet. May you always be so inclined.

May 13

You slept through your first earthquake tonight. About 10:00 p.m. I was downstairs watching the Giants and Braves go into extra innings when I felt the futon serving as our sofa begin to shimmy. My first thought was of a bus or large truck going by outside, but I remembered we live on a quiet residential street now, and the shimmy turned into a shake, and then a rumble, and I knew it was an earthquake.

Your mom had just gotten out of bed to pee and she called my name from the top of the stairs. I said, "That's an earthquake, baby."

It was the strongest one I've felt in some time, a 5.2 by early reports. Over 6.0 on the Richter scale begins to get frightening. 7+ and you are looking at major damage and possibly loss of life in a large metropolitan area like San Francisco.

If you are ever in an earthquake, remember, the bad ones keep building, getting stronger as the seconds pass. Tonight's lasted maybe five seconds. If you are in a bad one, do not run outside. The best thing to do is get in a doorway, where the structural supports of the building will protect you from crumbling walls and falling objects. If you can't get to a doorway, look for a heavy table to crawl under, get in a fetal position, and cover your head with your arms.

Even though we live on one of the planet's most famous tectonic fault lines, the odds of you ever getting killed or injured in an earthquake here are very, very minute. And in a way, quakes like the one tonight are exhilarating—it reminds you this earth is alive, with power far greater than anything mankind could ever devise. It helps keep you humble and attuned to the preciousness of life.

It does me, anyhow.

May 27

I'm not sure if I've put it to you this way yet, but I've been telling people for a couple of months now: you are really starting to connect the dots.

You are well on your way to knowing your ABCs; know A is for apple, B is for ball, C is for cat, J is for Janice, L is for Lofton (and Lonnie, of course)—and you can pick the letters off of the refrigerator perfectly.

You keep a running commentary going about your day and all the things you are seeing and doing, in fact, sometimes I wish you would shut the heck up, but that's my problem. You just learned how to talk and I shouldn't begrudge you the pleasure of trying out your new skills. I hope one day you will understand the wisest people keep their eyes and ears and hearts open, and they keep their mouths shut.

We've had a little shift in your routine of late. You are such an active dude, and now we have a yard to play in, with lots of dirt and bugs and room for you to run around and tumble in the grass and get yourself thoroughly coated in filth. So in the late afternoons, when playtime is over and I'm doing something about dinner, you take a bath. After that, it's dinner, some playing around the table, then stories in "the big night-night," a few more in your room, and lights out.

Mom and I do a pretty good job of sharing the bathing and bedtime activities, but my sense of it is you enjoy those things more with her than you do with me. I love reading to you, though, and we do get some good cuddly time together. These days your favorite books are *Where the Wild Things Are*, by Maurice Sendak, and *The Lorax*, by Dr. Seuss. We've got a bunch of others you love, too: one about baby animals, another about a hungry caterpillar, and a fun counting book called *Hippos Go Berserk*.

Sometimes when I'm reading to you, you take the book from me and say, "Lofton's turn." You sit there with the book open in your lap, ready to read, obviously unable just yet to decode the words printed on the page. But you sure can describe what you see, and you can remember certain keywords or phrases and where they go in the story, which just amazes me.

I'm unsure whether my amazement comes from an expectation you'd be less astute in recognizing the nature of the world around you or from the great joy I feel in seeing how naturally you assimilate all the things and people and experiences you encounter. But amazed I am, and before I go into full cheerleader mode, I'm going to bid you a good evening.

Midnight approaches at the end of the Memorial Day weekend and I'm tired. We had a big housewarming bash on Saturday, with over fifty people, thirteen kids (from eight months to eleven years), tons of food, live music, and a new Bar-B-Que. You had a great time with your friends, who are beginning to become numerous. We had fun showing off the new house to our friends and a few new neighbors and now we can settle in here for the next phase of our lives together. I'm glad you are with us, Lofton; I'm glad the three of us are all together.

August 20

I've been thinking of writing so much these past weeks and just haven't found or made the time to do it. Often enough something you'd say or do, some feeling I'd get in a moment with you would spark my resolve to mention it here. But I've also been wanting to give you a sense of all the changes our move and these days have put in motion. Because even as you are changing before our very eyes—you now see yourself as something different than a baby (and you are so sweet and gentle with them)—our family is undergoing a great shift.

I have sold Nickie's to a cousin, who you met in Florida when the two of us went to Miami. He is young and smart and full of energy and ideas, and I think he could be very good for the club. I am so very glad to have the end of my days at Nickie's in sight; as good as it's been to me, and despite the income from it on which I'll no longer be able to depend. My hope now is for D and I to sell the whole building by next spring and to be free from my ties to the Lower Haight.

Am I being shortsighted in my haste to leave there? Twenty years from now, will you read this with the Lower Haight having become a bustling, high-rent district full of life's most beautiful, fun, creative people—and rue me for having sold your birthright out from under you?

Well, I'll tell ya Lofton, right now it's a bustling low-rent district full of the entire slice of life, and you have spent a great deal of your first two years down there, soaking up all the energy, sights and sounds and vibes that make the place what it is. You are known in the Lower Haight. And you will carry with you always whatever one day may be cool or valuable about it.

As for me, twelve years is enough; it's time for me to move on.[19]

So the thing that inspired me to sit and tap the keyboard tonight was something you said today that must be recorded for posterity. After you woke from your afternoon nap, the two of us were sitting on the sofa in the living room. On the TV, a videotape played, showing me playing music last Thursday with the New Electric Band, a group of fellows I've been playing with for about a month or two. You know the TV well, I'm somewhat sorry to say, even though you seem to appreciate higher quality programming over much of the dreck to be found on it, and you have a varied and active life beyond it. But you have never

---

[19]   The young cousin and his business partner didn't turn out to be the answer at Nickie's. In their defense, it's never easy to take the reins of an organization as established and well-known as our little bar had become. My partners and I had a helluva time when we took it over from Miss Nickie, who'd run it for thirty years before us, creating a social focal point for the predominantly Black, working-class, Lower Haight/Western Addition neighborhood. The neighborhood was changing, though, when we got there in 1989, and through a lot of effort, long days and nights, community outreach, and marketing, we transformed it from a wild, speakeasy BBQ joint into a jumping, cutting-edge dance club. In 2002, the neighborhood wasn't changing so much as San Francisco itself was. A lot of fallout remained from the Dot-Com bust of the previous year, but the city was on its inexorable path to a cultural identity rooted in technology and obscene wealth disparity, and the new guys couldn't figure out what their business needed to make that transition. It didn't help that they ignored everything I tried to pass on to them on the marketing side, on top of failing to take advantage of new marketing opportunities brought about with the rise of the internet. After a little more than a year, when they'd fallen behind on paying taxes and were unable to make the final payment in the deal by which they'd acquired the club, I was forced to take it back and run it again myself for another nine months before we were able to find a buyer for the business and building together. Today, Nickie's is still there, incarnated as an Irish sports bar, for which there has always been room for another in San Francisco. The Lower Haight has not really changed much in the last twenty years, either: still diverse, still largely working-class. I go into Nickie's now and again and though the vibe is very, very different from the vibe in my decade there, I still sense the spirit of Miss Nickie and hear echoes of all the incredible nights of music I hosted there in the 1990s.

seen me on TV. And the tape quality was not, shall we say, pristine. I cued the tape to "Viva Lofton," but that night it was our final number, so, at the beginning I thanked some people and didn't go immediately into the verse. As the tape began to play, I asked you, "Who is that?" You looked at me without hesitation and said, "Elvis."

I was stunned. So I asked you again and you confirmed you thought you were seeing Elvis. That in itself would be something noteworthy enough. But what you did next made waves of love reverberate through my being.

As the song went into the verse and you recognized it as "Viva Lofton," you looked at me with bright eyes and a big smile and said, "That's Daddy!" It makes me so happy you love music, so happy you love my music, and I hope music will fill your life always.

August 30

Now you climb into and out of your crib. It's a day your Mom and I have been anticipating a while and, I guess, as is said, there's no turning back. You've surmounted your fundamental boundary. Your desires are no longer subject to the restraint of physical perimeters—you are free to venture forth in search of whatever might draw you from the comfort and security of your den, your nest, your home, from that which you know and in which you find solace. Look out world, here's Lofton!

August 31 (1:40 a.m.)

When I first sat at the computer tonight and opened this file, I happened to read some entries I made in the month or two before you were born. I ended up reading well past your first birthday before actually managing to start banging out this entry.

I haven't made it a practice to reread past entries, other than the most immediate one or two for copy editing purposes, so I was pleased to encounter my own vulnerabilities and to affirm the early indications of your magnificence.

One thing I noticed was a strong portion of those entries from two years ago came at 3:00 or 4:00 in the morning. Another was, I was already then beginning to think about Life Beyond Nickie's. Well, you'll note tonight's entry began well before 3:00 a.m., and I can tell you we've begun to approach Life Beyond Nickie's. The new guys are going to thrive there; Nickie's is going to thrive under them. That is my feeling.[20]

It's been only two weeks and they are yet very young men, but I do believe we've done a good thing—we've passed the baton well. Tonight I went down there, as is my Friday custom, and never got behind the bar. I enjoyed watching the crowd build and groove to the DJ's ministrations, enjoyed watching my cousin begin to take ownership of his bar. I definitely enjoyed walking out of there at 12:30 a.m. Soon, I'm sure, I'll be able to fully let go and not go down there at all, but for now I'm happy with the fact I'll finish this entry and be in bed before 2:30.

The story, of course, is I'm selling Nickie's because operating a nightclub is incompatible with parenting. Or, to be more precise, it's incompatible with my idea of parenting. I don't feel I can be the father I'd like to be and also be the nightclub operator I need to be. And while I've made a small success of operating a nightclub the past ten years, I hope to make a greater success of parenting in the next ten years. As you will learn, however, there is almost always more to the story. Yes, I want to be a good father. I also want to be a happy man. And I haven't been happy in the Nickie's milieu for some time.

A measure of my unhappiness lies in a disconnect between my spiritual values and the fact that I make a living selling alcohol. Of course, it's

---

[20]   See footnote 19. Oops.

not just alcohol I'm selling—I'm selling an opportunity for immersion in the joy and ecstasy of music and dance, and community—which certainly does align with my spiritual values. But the alcohol can be a problem. Some people can't handle it at all. Some people can't handle it sometimes. Given enough of it, everyone gets sloppy and loud and breaks things and hurts themselves and hurts others.

I have to get out of that place, I know.

Whether I'll end up being a good father is yet very much up in the air.

September 5

You caught your first bug today. I didn't get that good a look at it, but it appeared to have wings, which made it a noteworthy score. You've been interested in bugs, butterflies, and other winged & crawly things for some time, but would often recoil at their quick movements whenever you'd get near one. Recently you have been enjoying the programming on a television network called Animal Planet, in particular the exploits and adventures of a bold and charismatic young fellow by the name of Jeff Corwin.

Jeff travels all over the globe in search of everything from snakes to spiders to monkeys, crocodiles, and whales.

He's a fine person for you to emulate, in my view, because he treats the animals and their environment with great respect.

I'm pleased to see you exploring your world here at home, where you love to play in the backyard, running around the little patch of lawn, climbing in the dogwoods and junipers, playing intently with your fleet of trucks and planes in the little square of dirt by the deck. If I have my way you'll have lots of opportunities to play in the natural world, to explore everything you find interesting there during the next several years of your life.

As a kid, I was never much of a bug man, nor was I big on catching frogs or snakes, but I've come to appreciate and respect the natural world a great deal as an adult, and I'm looking forward to the the ways I may get to experience its wonders anew through your adventures and discoveries.

November 11

I am remiss in having failed to mention Liz (pronounce: leez), who has been your and Lyla's caretaker the last couple of months. She's a very sweet girl with lots of energy and loves to play with you at the gym and the playground. She helps you with art projects on rainy days, and is making a wonderful, supportive, active contribution to your development.

We, your mom and I and Lyla's parents, feel very fortunate to have had her come into our lives and I hope you will have some memories of her as you grow older, for she will have shaped you in many important ways.

You are finding yourself in your world now, showing mastery of the many physical skills you will need to thrive in life, also testing the wide range of emotional responses we humans are capable of. Your personality is filled with humor, curiosity, and playful determination, and you seem to be at home in any environment. You love to ride the Muni streetcar and the bus, and you love running round and round in circles, me chasing you, chasing me, in the house, in the yard, in the park, and the playground. We roll and tumble and wrestle on the floor and in our big bed–and your mom sometimes thinks we play too rough.

But I gather from your smiles and your giggles, and the gleam in your eyes, you are enjoying yourself as much as I am.

December 22

Here we are nearly at the end of the year. Seems like such a short while ago you were dressed in your skeleton outfit for Halloween, trick-or-treating with Lyla and Clare here in the neighborhood, and getting your first real introduction to candy. You love your chocolate, to be sure.

Now it's Christmas and you've a fondness for candy canes. But I don't detect any overly obsessive behavior about the stuff, so we're happy to let you have it as a treat now and again. You eat a pretty well-rounded diet I guess, save for what I might think is a shortage of green vegetables—but you'll really need their nutrients more a bit later in life.

For now, the cheese and potatoes and rice and bananas, tofu, cereal, eggs, and pasta you thrive on give you plenty of energy to explore your world and test your physical capabilities, all of which are expanding for you in leaps and bounds. You are a strong and fearless, good-hearted person, Lofton, yet you do not lord yourself over anyone or any place. You are adapting well to using manners in communicating with people and even when you have the inevitable meltdowns that come with realizing the cruel hard nature of life, you soon find something to soothe your pain, something to bring a smile to your lips and new light to your eyes.

The coming year promises to be pivotal in many ways. The world beyond our secure and happy home is in great tumult and deep uncertainties fill the air. In America, the economy is in the third year of a contraction that has seen many billions of dollars erased from bank accounts and balance sheets across the land.[21] This past year we saw the three largest corporate bankruptcy filings in our history; personal bankruptcies continue to climb and consumer debt is at an all-time high. Unemployment is on the rise, and so are prices, which is never a good combination, and while the optimism that is an American hallmark remains undaunted, it seems more people may be starting to fear the future than to look forward to it.

Adding to the malaise is our government's ill-advised belligerence toward Iraq. Iraq is a country in the Middle East governed in recent times by a horrible tyrant named Saddam Hussein. Let it never be disputed: he is a bad man who has done much evil in this world. The country he rules also happens to hold much of the world's proven reserves of oil, on which the machinery of our industrial economy runs. It seems the decision has been made at the highest levels of our government that we must maintain access to those oil reserves at all cost, so we have mounted a massive international public relations campaign to justify and seek approval for our intention to invade Iraq and oust Saddam Hussein from power.

Of course many thousands of innocent (mostly Iraqi) people will die in the process and our government will spend many billions of dollars that might otherwise have been spent on trying to improve life in America more directly, but few people in power feel the need to address that particular issue.

---

[21] In real-time writing I referred to what we were then experiencing as a "contraction" when, in due time, everyone knew it as a recession, though a mere prelude to The Great Recession that would wallop the nation in 2008. Coming in the next section of this book, you'll read more of my real-time assessments of this interesting period, when I wrote much less about and for you than I did about broader topics and mainly for myself.

It makes me angry and sad to see our so-called leaders betray the promise and idealism of the American way and I'm afraid things in our country may become dangerous and violent in the coming years.[22]

I guess I can only hope to teach you the true values that make up the American way and pray enough of your generation learns similar lessons at home so you can lead yourselves out of the mess we may well be leaving you.

---

[22] Hello, January 6, 2021.

2003

March 15

Nearly three months later, little has changed. You have grown larger, louder, and more expressive in your reflections of the world around you.

The wider world has remained in chaos; the United States is on the brink of war with Iraq. I have been trying to take advantage of tumultuous times to create capital by trading more actively in the stock and commodities markets. Who knows what may come to pass, but I hope to at least keep our family in a position to maintain both the security of a home and the freedom to travel.

Trading capital markets would be seen as a speculative and ill-advised pursuit in many societies—perhaps you will know a society where they play a less defining role than they do here today.

My feeling is you would benefit from the difference. But I live in the here and now, and for a person who is unwilling to take a position as a cog in the machinery of a rigid, industrial, impersonal social economy, the road to security and comfort is fraught with risk and uncertainty.

You will find many people respond to risk and uncertainty by taking comfort in the known, the familiar, the sure thing. Others see risk as an opportunity to discover the unknown, extraordinary thing that may bring about real change, real improvement, and a realization of the best things life has to offer. I am of the latter camp, as you might surmise. Only time will tell whether my approach is effective.

Meanwhile, you are becoming a full-fledged member of the community, complete with your own desires and demands, none of which you have yet seen fit to suppress whenever they might come to mind. You are still spending lots of time with Lyla and Liz and you have recently solidified your friendship with Raleigh, our neighbor across the street.

About a month ago you moved from your crib to a "big boy" bed and you have been making progressive efforts at responding to your defecatory urges by going to the toilet instead of in your diaper. Many boys do not get this convention of civilized behavior under control until four years of age or more. You have had some very positive experiences in the past several weeks, though you also seem to be a little taken aback by this transition to personhood. It remains to be seen whether you will get the poop thing down in the next year. Meanwhile, we've begun to change fewer diapers, and that is a good thing.

May 6

Perhaps you may imagine me thinking often of this journal, watching you do some silly little thing to cause me to think you are a genius, or a warrior, a criminal, or just an ordinary three-year-old, and rueing the fact of my only-occasional entries.

I would love to be compiling something here with the richness of entries made weekly at a minimum, sometimes daily in stretches—but it is what it is. So when I do eventually sit down and re-read the most previous entry or two, I'm often amazed at how the things I was writing about seven weeks ago (in this instance) are still relevant in their way. It's a good way of reminding myself, and perhaps illustrating to you, how slowly things change over time.

I'll give you a brief synopsis of what the past seven weeks have meant vis-a-vis the things I said in March.

Not that it's necessarily the most important thing, but you are 90 percent toilet-trained, dude! You sleep in a diaper at night but spend the rest of your time doing a great job of letting us know when you have to pee or poop. You are even mostly capable of attending to your own basic hygiene around this aspect of your development.

Your cousin was babysitting you several weeks ago when the two of you were temporarily locked in the backyard of the house. You told him you had to pee and so he showed you how to pee in the grass, which you now take some pleasure in doing from time to time. Your mom and I even watched you take a substantial poop in the yard a few days ago.

(I have very few concerns about your oneness with Nature at this point.)

Your differentiation of yourself as an independent actor is also well along this last month-and-a-half. You have begun to get impulsively physical, especially in situations where, as I often refer you to the old Rolling Stones song, *You Can't Always Get What You Want.*

This has caused us to begin introducing discipline into your life.

Our early method is the Time-Out. We let you know you are doing something unacceptable, give you an opportunity to recognize that and change your behavior, and if you fail to do so, we remove you from the present arena, most often to your room—but if we are out in public, to a nearby restroom. You generally wail and moan for the three minutes we keep you sequestered, but you tend to be much more in control of yourself afterwards. We are very hopeful this technique will spare all of us the difficulties of an undisciplined childhood for you.

We celebrated your third birthday a few weeks ago with a little party on a Saturday morning here. Your friends were here with their parents and your cousin and his pals stopped by to wish you well. We had The Lizard Lady come with a dozen exotic snakes and lizards and a rare South American tortoise for everyone to see. You were up at the front of the room with The Lizard Lady, and you got to handle all the animals, which you seemed to enjoy in a very dignified, respectful way. I hope the photographs and video I shot from that day survive for you to really appreciate one day.

The United States ended up invading Iraq in the beginning of April, and after some initial bad weather and a week or so of grumbling about strategy, proceeded to topple the Saddam Hussein regime in three weeks. Many thousands of Iraqi soldiers and civilians were killed, some 30,000 bombs were dropped on the country, and dozens of American soldiers were killed by their own comrades in the process— but the Iraqi oil fields have been made safe for exploitation by Western industrial interests.

Saddam Hussein and the weapons of mass destruction with which he was purportedly threatening our security and way of life are nowhere to be found. There is talk of establishing a democratic government there, which, if successful, will spell the beginning of the end of the Arab royal family's rule in much of the Middle East. However, the task may well be beyond our country's ability and attention to get the job done, in which case the most volatile region on the planet will grow more hostile, more chaotic, and bring mankind ever closer to looking its own extinction in the face. It's not a completely lovely world you've arrived in, I'm afraid.

Making matters worse, on the home front, I've made some abysmal trades in the stock and commodities markets in the last seven weeks, wiping out almost 40 percent of the assets I had to invest. I made very risky trades in an attempt to reap very grand profits in a time of volatility and uncertainty, and thus far I have been proven very wrong by the markets.

I do honestly believe my outlook may yet be vindicated, however.

Whether I stand to profit by my outlook remains very much in doubt at this juncture. I'm betting against a lot of the interests our government was installed to protect, and though I truly believe the forces of nature will do them in, I can only hope to create some capital for us out of the sea change I believe is coming to our society.

Meanwhile, we are living on savings and credit until I receive the final payment for Nickie's in August. The next three months will be very tight for us and I'm afraid it will bring lots of stress and anxiety into our home life. But your mom and I are both working hard in yoga and meditating to focus on what is truly important for all of us: having love and open hearts for one another and for the wide world around us, and dedicating ourselves to living that love and openness in every small way, every single day.

I remain, as is my wont, optimistic.

July 13

I wonder whether you will have any memory of a day like today. For me it began with murmurings of you and your mom downstairs discussing whether you would be coming to the table to eat your breakfast or watch superhero cartoons on the television. Because Mom was getting ready to leave for work your insistence on superhero watching won out, at least until she rousted me from bed and I made my way down to my first cup of coffee.

Soon we had hashbrowns, steak, eggs, fruit juice, and cereal on the breakfast table and I loved watching you sit so tall and straight in your little chair at your little table, eating purposefully, quietly, storing the energy you'd unleash later as we made our way through the day.

You enjoyed cartoons a while through the morning:

Superman, Batman, Scooby Doo, some Power Rangers, Tom & Jerry, too, while I played music in the kitchen, working on a new song and an old cover. We went upstairs a couple of times to put on epic pillow fights on Mom's & my bed, and after hiding out as Buzz Lightyear and Spiderman in the cave of our bedsheets, we got dressed and went into the garage to get the big blue tent I use for camping in the great outdoors.

Soon we had it pitched in the backyard and all the superheroes were inside, where you and I hid a bit from the hot summer sun and indulged in our fantasies—something that comes so naturally to you, and which I am working hard to rediscover from my own childhood.

Once the tent/cave base was secured, we moved back into the garage to activate the red super transporter, my 1960 MGA roadster. We were soon off into the ease of a sunny San Francisco Sunday afternoon. We spun around the neighborhood a bit and then motored over to CW's (an artist/friend) house and studio across from Precita Park.

After C and I caught up with each other, you went down to the playground and swung so high on the swings, climbed ladders, slid down slides, ran and jumped and made friends with a couple of kids playing there, too—it seemed you were having such fun, exploring your world, being in it, making it your own. I was only as much a part of it as you wished for me to be. I honored and respected your expressions of autonomy and forgot for a moment you are only a little over three years old.

Last weekend Mom had to take you to the emergency room for an ear infection and she told me the doctor who saw you was so very impressed with the way you handled yourself—precocious, he called you, I believe—and I knew today, not for the first time, but in a fresh, palpable way I haven't considered in a long while, it is going to be so fun to grow up with you.

I hope it doesn't creep you out that I am reliving my own childhood through yours, but somehow it seems only yours can validate my experience of my own. As I see you understand and master your world I accept and appreciate how I have understood and mastered my own.

You are beginning to confide in me, to tell me how you want me to be, what you want to do, where you want to go, and even more importantly, how you feel about the things we are doing all the time. Mostly you turn to Mom for comfort and assurance, for license and approval. She is your main source of security, encouragement, and refuge. But you and I are developing a relationship and a bond I hope we can find strength in for many years to come.

I am very content in our life together right now, Lofton, and I can only hope you are able to draw some glimmer of a memory of this idyllic time later in your life.

These are the Good Old Days.

PART 3

I JUST HAVE TO SAY

THE BLOGGING YEARS: 2003 - 2008

*The following section consists of a selection of posts from a blog
I began writing shortly after the terrorist attacks on 9/11, and
which I maintain today, called* I Just Have To Say. *The most
consistent updates came in the George W. Bush years, between
2003 and 2008, though I rekindled the blogging spark again in
2010 and have updated it more or less intermittently since.*

2003

December 14

They finally bagged the Butcher of Baghdad. Let's hear, once again, three cheers for the Red, White, and Blue.

Seriously, this is a historic event for which the brave men and women of the United States' Armed Forces, who deserve the commendation of all freedom-loving people in this world, not to mention the eternal gratitude of the long-suffering citizens of Iraq.

But, much as the "Mission Accomplished" banner and President Bush's infamous "major combat operations are over" statements aboard the USS Abraham Lincoln proved empty symbols of our collective desire, we would all do well to not read the capture of Saddam Hussein for the end of harm and danger to U.S. troops in Iraq, or the guarantee of a peaceful, free, and fair society for the Iraqi people.

Gazing upon Saddam's haggard, disheveled countenance this morning I was put in mind of nothing so much as a fox at the end of a hunt, just before the dogs rip its broken, worn-out body to shreds. And surely his fate will be similar. He'll stand trial for his crimes against humanity, though at this early date it remains unclear whether his tribunal will consist of Iraqi justices, American justices, or those of the International Criminal Court.

His nose will be rubbed in the prurient details of his heinous behavior and news outlets worldwide will breathlessly recount the depths of his depravity for audiences all-too-willing to revel in catharsis over his presence in the dock instead of making all-too-hard and complicated choices about what to do with all the other foxes remaining in the desert.

And then he will hang, or be shot, or gassed, or electrocuted, or poisoned—but surely he will die.

And then, what, ladies and gentlemen of the jury? Will lions lie down with lambs? Swords be beaten into ploughshares? Will Israelies find common cause with Palestinians, Syrians, Jordanians, Saudis, Egyptians, Lebanese? With any one of those peoples?

Will Islamic fundamentalists cease preaching hate and death for America? Will suicide bombers roam the earth no more? Perhaps hell will freeze over and the desert will bloom with a billion flowers, or at least one for every victim of Saddam's brutality.

Fascism did not die in the bunker with Adolf Hitler, nor with the trial and execution of Nuremburg's defendants. Racism did not die with the admission of James Lee Meredith to the University of Mississippi in 1962, or with the signing of the Civil Rights Act of 1964.

The fact of fascism's continued existence and rascism's stubborn presence in the world does not diminish the importance of those historic events, just as the virulence of terrorism and the seeming impasse between Arabic and Western worldviews do not render the capture of Saddam Hussein a trivial matter.

But, in the immortal words of Karen and Richard Carpenter, "We've only just begun."

December 29

George W. Bush is going to wish he never heard of a spider hole.[23]

Once the initial *huah* over Saddam Hussein's capture began to recede under continuing reverberations from suicide bombings, coordinated insurgencies, and the steadily climbing death toll of American service personnel in Iraq, it became clear that one more thing the U.S. Administration didn't have a plan for was finding its Bogeyman alive.

During the long months on the lam Hussein spent growing that natty beard, Bush and his henchmen took pains to distance themselves from the idea that it made any difference whether Hussein was dead or alive. What mattered was the sparkly new freedom of the Iraqi people and the democratic light they would bring to the rest of the Arab world.

What mattered was raising funds and personnel from "coalition" countries to help with reconstruction.

What mattered was showing the world that U.S. hegemony is good medicine.

And then, there he was, looking for all the world just like any number of the raggedy souls I see every day in San Francisco's Tenderloin, or by the entrance to Golden Gate Park on Stanyan Street, or all up and

---

[23] A spider hole in military parlance is a type of camouflaged one-man foxhole, used for observation. It is typically a shoulder-deep, protective, round hole, often covered by a camouflaged lid, in which a soldier can stand and fire a weapon. A foxhole is usually deeper and designed to emphasize cover rather than concealment. On December 13, 2003, American forces captured Saddam Hussein hiding in what was characterized as a "spider hole" outside an Ad-Dawr farmhouse near his hometown of Tikrit.

down Haight Street and Market Street—hell, if Saddam had somehow managed to get here, they might never have found him.

But I digress. Find him they did, and bully for the forces of Good, as I said in a previous installment of this series. But now that he's been had, the question remains: What to do with the old dirty bastard?

He's been tried and convicted many times over in the courts of non-Arab world opinion. Heinous, despicable, inhuman, monstrous, unconscionable—those are some of the more genteel epithets with which he's been saddled over the years. Certainly many, many people in this world would think it quite all right if he were turned over to the Iraqi Kurds, say, to be summarily disemboweled and fed to dogs on international TV. However, as long as Rupert Murdoch has no say in the matter, that is not the likely scenario.

The Bush administration has been pointedly circumspect in offering scenarios of its own regarding any effort to bring the former dictator of Iraq to justice. In fact, after the initial blush of euphoria at his capture, after the fun with his medical and dental exams, his shave and his haircut, Saddam Hussein and his fate have been oddly out of the news. And if they can help it at all, that's just the way Bush and his crew will want to keep it.

The Hague, a dreary city in northern Europe, is home to The International Tribunal for the Prosecution of Persons Responsible for Serious Violations of International Humanitarian Law Committed in the Territory of the Former Yugoslavia since 1991 (ICTY).

The star defendant currently in the dock before the ICTY is Slobodan Milosevic, Yugoslavia's former leader, who has been called to account for some of the many horrific atrocities visited upon predominately Muslim citizens of Bosnia, Croatia, and Yugoslavia during the decade of the 1990s.

The ICTY is heir to the community of nations' best intentions to create lawful forums for the fair adjudication of war crimes and violations of International Humanitarian Law, which began with Allied oversight of the Nazi War Crimes Trials at Nuremberg in 1945, and the International Military Tribunal for the Far East, which tried twenty-eight high-ranking Japanese defendants in Tokyo from April, 1946 to November, 1948.

Since the founding of the ICTY, similar tribunals have been established to investigate and prosecute crimes and atrocities for Rwanda, East Timor, and Sierra Leone. There is a fascinating article detailing all of this and much more in the January 2004 issue of Harper's Magazine.[24]

What struck me in reading the article, and what has no doubt occurred to the brains of the Bush operation, is that, when Saddam Hussein is tried for this crimes, a few very prickly decisions must be made, in addition to the obvious ones about where and how to try him.

As Lesser says in the article, in a footnote:

> *The several years of both direct and indirect preparation involved in, for example, marshaling adequate admissible evidence and finding witnesses is but one issue. Others include whose notion of a "fair" trial will prevail, and whether the trial is to deal with almost twenty-five years of International Humanitarian Law and human-rights abuses or ought to be a brief proceeding limited in its scope. If the latter, victims families are certain to raise passionate objections. A trial of broad scope, on the other hand, would drag on for several years. And it is easy to imagine that much would be made of active U.S. support of Hussein's regime during his country's conflict with Iran, that the "legality" of the*

[24] Lesser, Guy, Lena Dunham, Rana Dasgupta, and Sallie Tisdale. "[Article] War Crime and Punishment, By Guy Lesser." *Harper's Magazine*, January 1, 2004. https://harpers.org/archive/2004/01/war-crime-and-punishment/.

U.S. invasion would be vigorously contested by the defendant(s), and that every effort possible would be made to play to the region's anti-American audience, portraying Hussein as both a martyr, struggling to defend Islam from the West, and something of a pawn, turned upon and betrayed by his former ally, the United States. Doubtless, too, some attempt would be made not only to portray the current Bush agenda for the Middle East in a sinister light but also to implicate the United States during the period prior to Iraq's invasion of Kuwait, perhaps even in the role of an accomplice that supplied and trained Hussein's armed forces while turning a blind eye to IHL crimes they were fully aware of and might have done something to prevent.

The great Hollywood director John Ford once said: "When it's a choice between writing the story and writing the myth, write the myth."

In the present case, George Bush, if he even bothers to wrap his mind around the situation at all, must wish either that Saddam Hussein had been a more fanatical believer in Islam and the promise of Heaven made to its martyrs, or that those American bombs had been smarter.

Then, he could have ridden the myth of Saddam Hussein as evil incarnate into the sunset of history. Now, unfortunately, he'll have to watch and listen, along with the rest of us, to how the story isn't quite that simple and to how the United States of America has plenty of blood on its hands to go along with the lust for oil in its heart.

2004

March 20

According to the secretary of defense, in an op-ed piece published in yesterday's New York Times, the real reason for the United States' "adventure" in Iraq (able now, finally, on the one-year anniversary of its onset, to be revealed): Baghdad might—some fifty years hence—be like Seoul, Korea.

That, on a table in the office of the secretary of defense fifty years from now, a nighttime satellite surveillance photograph of the middle east will boast, where Iraq is today, a place "ablaze in light, the light of freedom."

Give Donald Rumsfeld credit for the Big Picture View.[25]

Let us set aside for a moment, as the secretary so happily wishes we would, everything he and the other spokespersons for the Bush administration told the American people and the world in the "run-up" to our "adventure" in Iraq. He reminds us what a bad, bad man Saddam Hussein was (neglecting, however, to remind us how other U.S. administrations in which the secretary served, viewed and used the bad, bad man as an asset to advance our country's interests in the Middle East).

---

[25] Donald Henry Rumsfeld (born July 9, 1932) is a retired American politician. Rumsfeld served as Secretary of Defense from 1975 to 1977 under Gerald Ford, and again from January 2001 to December 2006 under George W. Bush. Between his terms as Secretary of Defense, he served as the CEO and chairman of several companies, which, as it turns out, tended to be profitable with the U.S. at war.

Let us set aside, for a moment, as the secretary so happily wishes we would, his being nailed on last Sunday's *Face the Nation* TV News program, telling a very different story about our "adventure" in Iraq than the one he wishes us to believe today.

He paints now our raison d'etre as something akin to the glory we achieved on the Korean peninsula fifty years ago, adding, in case the luster of that splendid little war isn't sufficient to make things clear, it's also a little like what we did for Germany, Japan, and Italy by putting down the last century's baddest, baddest man in World War II.

In Donald Rumsfeld's view, *This Is What We Do,* y'all.

But the secretary is mistaken.

This is different. I've alluded before to the proposition that freedom cannot be imposed or bestowed on people. Whatever may have been the dirty little particulars fueling the flames of war in Korea, the United States joined people willing to fight and die for their freedom against other, ideologically abhorrent people.

In World War II, people from many nations across the globe joined to combat and defeat two different though equally dangerous nationalist pathologies.

The fact is Donald Rumsfeld and the rest of the Bush administration don't know squat about the Iraqi people or what they want.

Clearly, a bunch of them were just fine with Saddam Hussein at the helm. For a whole other bunch, it's not so clear. There are those who are willing, for whatever their own personal reasons, to act as emissaries for The American Way, God bless 'em. On the whole, everything about our "adventure" in Iraq would indicate our motive has always been exactly what the secretary admitted yesterday: to bring "the light of freedom."

Sounds like a good thing, right?

I guess we'll see.

Daniel Ellsberg, and others who have a contemporary understanding of the way our government operates, assures us we'll have many years and plenty of additional casualties (not to mention the hundreds of billions of dollars we'll spend supporting and preserving our emissaries who do not become casualties) with which to calculate the headline Times editors gave to Mr. Rumsfeld's exhortation today: The Price of Freedom in Iraq.[26]

I think we are overpaying. And we are asking our children, and their children, to overpay for whatever the nighttime satellite picture of the middle east is going to look like in fifty years.

If we have the hundreds of billions of dollars to spend (reasonable doubt about which exists), we should spend it not on a war on terrorism, not on a war on drugs, rather on a war on fear, on a war on hopelessness, and on worry, and want.

We should spend our money, our hearts, our last dying breaths on a war on ignorance, a war on hubris, a war on war.

I can hear the cries now: "Appeaser!"

But appeasement is a big red herring in the debate over the resources we have committed to the war on terrorism and to our bringing "the light of freedom" to the middle east.

Whatever the conflict between the trappings of modern, mostly western, mostly Judeo-Christian, mostly capitalist civilization, and

---

26   Cooper, Bob. 2012. "Is Daniel Ellsberg Right ... Again?" SFGATE. *San Francisco Chronicle*. January 29. https://www.sfgate.com/magazine/article/Is-Daniel-Ellsberg-Right-Again-2788667.php.

modern radical Islam—the world is not faced today with a "choice" about something as heinous or menacing or truly "imminent" as was Hitler and Nazi totalitarianism.

We ought to be able to marginalize a few raving clerics in the hills of Asia minor without mortgaging the farm, don't you think?

We as a nation, as a freedom-loving people, are being stupid. We are being willfully ignorant about confronting things we believe to be wrong in the world. We are allowing a handful of raving despots in our own midst to plunder our vast resources and squander whatever good will remains of our previous efforts to champion the cause of freedom in the world, while they and their closest friends enrich personal fortunes in the bargain.

We are allowing our leaders to assume the role of the world's policeman, the world's scold, the world's interpreter of the word of God. It's as if we woke up one day and found ourselves being ruled by a band of Ayatollahs.

I say we can do better. I say we can approach the problem of radical Islam far more effectively and at a far better cost in lives and resources than George W. Bush, Dick Cheney, Donald Rumsfeld, and Paul Wolfowitz would have us believe.

First, however, we must abandon war as the answer. We must demand our leaders tell us the truth. And we must turn the current bunch of "crooked, you know, lying" leaders out of office immediately.

June 8

I was having a perfectly fine weekend, one of those clear, windswept spates of the Northern California year when a high yellow sun just makes up for the frigid energy sweeping down from Alaska and you can feel the hairs on your skin prickle in shirtsleeves. Then, I heard Ronald Reagan had died.

I imagined then the warm and fuzzy reminiscences to come from the print and television media, the wistful nostalgia for "The Man Who Saved The World" we've seen the past few days.

I got to thinking about the truth of Mr. Reagan's presidency, about his willful ignorance of Saddam Hussein's and Osama bin Laden's terrorist potential; about his shameless embrace of some of the world's most corrupt and bloodthirsty despots—the Marcoses, Duartes, and Duvaliers; about his willingness to pretend the apartheid of the South African regime had no meaning; about his denial of the AIDS epidemic and his refusal to commit federal resources to combat or contain it.

I fumed to recall his duplicity in championing smaller, less intrusive government while presiding over the largest, most costly federal bureaucracy to date, and I wondered why, even at this remove, the vast majority of people seem unwilling to hold his leadership accountable for producing the greatest number of government officials ever to be jailed, indicted, or investigated for misconduct, malfeasance in office, and/or criminal activity.

I cringed to think of how his candidate for vice-president, George Bush the Elder, made a secret deal with Iranian militants to continue holding Americans hostage until after Mr. Reagan had a chance to unseat Jimmy Carter for the Presidency in 1980.

I was dumbfounded to explain the failure of our Constitutional processes to rectify his administration's begetting a completely lawless, unchecked, shadow government that sold arms to Iran, used the money to support terrorism in Latin America, and implicated our country's own intelligence agencies in an explosion of drug use among the nation's most vulnerable citizens.[27]

Mr. Reagan presided over a domestic Savings & Loan industry scandal that cost American taxpayers many billions of dollars—back when dollars were worth something—and committed the country to a course of developing a space-based missile defense system that, today, more than twenty years hence, continues to drain unconscionable resources from the Federal budget while providing no actual defense against an enemy that no longer exists.

I reeled from these bilious flashbacks as I stepped out of the shower and noticed an inspirational quotation we have hanging on the bathroom wall.

It speaks of having compassion for all beings and developing the heart, and I am delighted to find a way to finally accommodate the entirety of Ronald Wilson Reagan, the 40th President of the United States of America.

In my heart, without benefit of knowing him personally, I can accept the possibility that Mr. Reagan was a kind and decent man, that he believed in his own heart the goodness and rightness of his every official act, that he was convinced a pure, indomitable American spirit would create and sustain a rising standard of life for all peoples of the planet. Surely he alone is not to blame that such is not the case.

The great irony of seeing Mr. Reagan in that light lies in his death. For how could such a good, courageous, visionary man be made to suffer the ignominy and horror of a decade of dying that is the curse of Alzheimer's disease?

If the Buddhists are correct and every pain and hardship, every trial and tribulation, every burden and suffering endured in this lifetime

---

[27]   All of those things really happened. You can look it up.

purifies one's cosmic, karmic debt, Mr. Reagan has just made it a little ways toward becoming the mythic character some writers of history will try to relate.

October 28

From the "I Just Have To Say" Sports Desk

For eighty-six years, the Boston Red Sox aimed to win a World Series.

In this pursuit, they were not unlike any organized team in any league, playing any sport, in any nation, ever. Every sports team wants to win its League Championship.

Of course, it's one of the great things about organized sport that only one team can win it all in a given season. It relegates the rest, the vast majority—the masses—to annual disappointment. In this way, sports are like real life.

But the quest for a championship also creates a reason for the annual renewal of hope. In the world of sport, it is the reason to be.

For eighty-six years, the hopes of the Boston Red Sox and their fans were annually dashed. Many years, the dashing came early and with certainty. A few times, victory seemed tantalizingly close, only to squirt between someone's legs, or be otherwise led by the hand of fate to another team's locker room.

For eighty-six years, the Boston Red Sox' and their fans' annual disappointment was rooted in The Curse of the Bambino.

Bad ju-ju leftover from Boston's having traded away, in 1918, the once and future Sultan of Swat, Babe Ruth—who would go on to lead the New York Yankees to a decade of championships and establish himself as perhaps the greatest baseball player of all time—was said to doom the cradle of the American Revolution to perpetual baseball futility.

This year had begun to look like so many in the past eighty-six. The Red Sox battled their Yankees nemeses the entire season and were on the brink of elimination in the American League playoffs, when they began to write a new page in sports history.

Down 3-0 in a best-of-four playoff series with the Yankees, they confronted the first of sports history's maxims: No baseball team had ever forced even a seventh game after being down by three in a seven-game series.

But the Sox did it, taking four in a row from the Yankees. The final two wins they secured in New York, to renew the idea that anything is possible.

They went on to the World Series against the St. Louis Cardinals, who had won more regular season games than any team in baseball this year. The cursed Sox went on to smoke the Cards, winning four games in a row, the last two in St. Louis, to give proof to the idea that history is not dead.

And so this morning, vast numbers of people throughout the globe awaken to a new reality—and to lives unencumbered by "The Curse."

Among Boston Red Sox fans everywhere, and perhaps among some people who are not even particularly fans of the sport of baseball at all, there is a sense that justice can prevail, that their time can come, that all hope is not lost. The universe has revealed that optimism can be rewarded, even if it takes a long life to collect the reward.

Given the state of affairs beyond the sylvan fields of the baseball diamond, a Boston Red Sox World Series victory could not have come at a better time.

November 10

When I was a sophomore in college, a friend of mine's father came to town to watch a horse he owned run in the Louisiana Derby.

It was an exciting week. We got full privileges at the racetrack and spent lots of time hanging around the paddock with Dr. K and his horse trainer, watching Spartan Emperor get put through his paces, getting the inside dope on the mysterious world of high-stakes thoroughbred horse racing.

In the evenings, Dr. K took us to eat in some of New Orleans' finest restaurants and kept us up into the wee hours drinking sazeracs and smoking cigars, regaling us with tales of his thirty years buying and breeding racehorses. Losers and mediocre entries far outnumbered the winners, but a trip to the winner's circle, smiling for the cameras with the jockey sitting high in the saddle, made all the angst and the money invested worthwhile.

The morning of the Derby, I put on my only sport coat and a borrowed pair of semi-respectable shoes, hopped on the streetcar with my friend CK and our buddy CM, and headed for the track. We had box seats and a reserved table in the Clubhouse, with all of it on Dr. K's tab. Which was good, because I'd scraped together my last $50 to put on Spartan Emperor to win.

I felt good, in part because I'd seen the photo of CK standing in a winner's circle with Spartan Emperor's sire. Our horse came from good stock, and had already compiled some impressive finishes in his young career. If he did well today, talk was he'd be entered in the Kentucky Derby later that Spring.

But I was also feeling good because I liked The Life. Horse racing is all about passion and power, and that week I'd been awed by the

185

huge, yet delicate beasts over which all the fuss is made. I'd felt the trembling of the earth standing outside the rails, right on the track, when the horses came thundering by at frightening speed, snorting and flailing saliva. The trainers and the stable hands plied their paddock turf as a sovereign kingdom, but graciously welcomed our visits and our questions and our interest in their stories.

I liked the rich, spicy bite of good Cajun cuisine, the sweet desserts, and the bitter flavor of chicory in my coffee. I loved the breakfast Bloody Marys and the cold beer and freshly shucked oysters, the single malt scotch, and the late night sazeracs. I liked the pretty girls who sat at our table in the Clubhouse, friends of the trainer and the jockey. They were older than us, they were in that Life, and they made us feel welcome.

The field settled into the starting gates and with the bell, Spartan Emperor broke for the lead, and the rail, and I had him pegged in my binoculars. I started to feel a great anticipation like nothing I'd ever known. As they hit the eighth pole we started to chant, "Go Seven, Go Seven," or whatever number he was wearing, leading the field by a length and a half. Through the backstretch, he filled my eyes, striving, stretching, pulling into a lead now of over two lengths.

I began to jump up and down and tug on the arm of CK's jacket, screaming, "Come ON, Seven, COME ON, Seven!" I saw my $50 turning into bags of money as they rounded the Clubhouse turn.

And suddenly I lost him.

I took the binoculars from my face and scanned the pack coming down the home stretch. "Where'd he go?!" I cried, jamming the binoculars back in my sockets. "Where'd he go?!!!"

And like that, it was over. Spartan Emperor finished next to last in a race that lasted less than two minutes. My Fifty bucks vaporized.

Everything good and decadent and delicious about that week was sucked into an empty place in the pit of my stomach. I thought I was going to throw up right there.

The nearest I've come to feeling that way in the succeeding twenty-four years was when it dawned on me John Kerry was nowhere to be seen at the end of this election.

I'd been so sure of his victory, had seen it arriving so clearly through my media-goggles, right into the home stretch. But it vanished into a sea of red state electoral votes and a breathtaking three-million vote advantage in the popular count for Mr. Bush.

When Spartan Emperor lost in early 1980, I think I went back to my apartment to smoke fulminous quantities of pot and sleep until about two weeks before finals, when I knew I had to get up and do something if I was to stay in school. But I'm a grown-up now and, tempting though it is, I can't choose that option today.

We have serious problems with our electoral process, citizens, and if we smoke a bunch of dope (or drink a vat of whisky, or take Xanax, or Zoloft, or burn too much sage) and go to sleep here, we will pay hell getting our democracy back.

Thirty-four million people voted or had their votes "scanned" in this election, on machines offering no receipt, no record of each vote, nor any verifiable method of obtaining a recount in the case of uncertainty. Many of these machines were manufactured by a company whose titular head is an avowed vocal and financial supporter of Mr. Bush—and who had publicly "guaranteed" delivery of the Ohio vote to the incumbent.

Has the term "conflict of interest" lost all currency in the early going of the 21st century? Could any jurisdiction with a genuine interest in unfettered democracy use such machines in good conscience? Should such use be legal in a true democratic republic?

I was ready to capitulate. I mean, it was a long race for me.

I had started actively backing and contributing time and money to the Dennis Kucinich campaign in June of '03. It was an uphill, though gratifying battle all the way to the Democratic convention in September. My experience with that campaign gave me hope for (if not confidence in) our electoral process, hope for our possibilities as a society, and pride in the youth of this country.

At some point near the end, however, I began to let go, and started saying to myself and to my ideological sparring partners, "Fine, let's just count the votes."

Therein lies the rub. There is the matter of the aforementioned incredible three million vote margin in the count for Mr. Bush, together with the victory to be ratified by the Electoral College on December 13.[28]

Questions abound, however, about the accuracy of the reported totals, and about the transparency of the process by which those totals are certified.

A whole host of suspicious circumstances were reported in Florida, Ohio, Indiana, New Hampshire, and other states.

Members of Congress have moved to investigate whether people were wrongly prevented from voting, or if legitimate votes were miscounted or not counted at all. It is clear we need to know, so any wrongdoers can be held accountable, and to help prevent this from happening again.

---

[28]   The 2020 Election: "Hold my beer."

Feeling the echoes of the empty place inside me gonged by the election results last week, I lost faith in the ability of our electoral system to effectively convey, embody, or apply the will of the people to the problems we face at this juncture. A long look must be given to the methods by which we vote and tabulate our votes in this country.

While I don't advocate requiring every precinct in the land to use the same device, a uniform standard of collecting and tabulating votes must be agreed upon. A verifiable paper trail, something physical we can refer to in the event of dispute, ought to be a threshold requirement.

Whether the country truly has a war-mongering, gay-baiting, fundamentally repressed majority, whether we are truly split between those who connect hope and progress with liberal values or with conservative ones, election day ought not feel like a day at the races.

2005

July 12

Lewis H. Lapham, the Editor-in-Chief of one of America's smartest, most engaging monthlies, *Harper's*, thoroughly explicates in his July editorial the futility of blaming George W. Bush for everything. Mr. Bush is, of course, doing his level best to do what he's been told to do—project for the country, and the world, the "powers of the American imagination [and] the strength of the American spirit."

Insofar as we fail to recognize this, we "do ourselves a disservice, and dishonor the memory of the Alamo and P.T. Barnum."

Mr. Bush and his administration are but reflections of a democracy that would be wholly unrecognizable to Richard Nixon, let alone Franklin D. Roosevelt or Thomas Jefferson. Ben Franklin must certainly be spinning in his grave.

In the same issue of the magazine, Ken Silverstein chronicles the many mechanisms by which 15,584 separate "earmarks"—diversions of U.S. Treasury funds directed anonymously by members of both the House and Senate Appropriations Committees, often by single-line declarations buried in the massive appropriations bills that keep this beast of a nation flapping its wings and flaring its nostrils like none in the annals of recorded time—how that many "earmarks" worth a combined $32.7 billion were attached to appropriations bills in 2004.

These are figures that have doubled since the year 2000, and which amounted to just 2000 earmarks and $10.6 billion in 1998.

And there's all kinds of unseemly lobbyist-campaign contribution-legislation-private beneficiary kinda crap going on—on both sides of the aisle.

Free markets indeed.

Our obvious overwhelming military superiority against any possible combination of other nations in this world cannot protect us from the rot we've spawned from within. We may be destined, despite the patriotism of each and every last one of us, to fare no better than the Greeks and Romans, on whose example we've based both our institutions and our comportment—despite the self-avowed religious foundation.

And yet, we have mechanisms for addressing these things. In fact, an important one has been on the books since 1789 and—surprise—the Bush administration and many of your favorite name brands and/or stock holdings would like to see it changed, pronto.

It's called the Alien's Action for Tort, and it grants United States courts jurisdiction to hear any claim for the violation of international law—the audacity of which should surprise no one in the current administration.

Lately it's been invoked to produce a Supreme Court ruling regarding its applicability, and it inspired the American oil conglomerate UNOCAL to settle for tens of millions of dollars the claims of Burmese villagers enslaved and abused by Burmese officials at UNOCAL's behest while the company completed a gas pipeline through the remote, little-known buddhist nation.

Currently, the likes of Coca-Cola, ChevronTexaco, and ExxonMobile face litigation, and victims of 9/11 along with Afghan and Iraqi victims of torture at U.S. prison camps have sued several military contractors, as well as Secretary of Defense Donald Rumsfeld under the law.

USC 28 IV 85 Sec.1350[29] is decried by the National Foreign Trade Council as a law that could "seriously damage the world economy and discourage companies from rebuilding countries like war-torn Iraq."

Fancy that.

September 1

It's been a rather impressive millennium on the natural disaster front.

Major earthquakes in Gujarat, India (2001) and Iran (2003) killed over 40,000 people, and in December 2004, the strongest earthquake anywhere in the world in over forty years, a 9.0 temblor beneath the Indian Ocean, spawned massive tidal waves that devastated coastal areas of Sri Lanka, Thailand, India, and Sumatra, killing nearly 300,000 people.

Presumably, many animals and other living things perished in these things as well, but let's stay focused on the human factor, since we are the only species on the planet to entertain the notion we might:

a) have any thing to do with natural disasters; and/or
b) be able to do anything about them.

Wildfires have long plagued the American West: 2003 saw California's worst in a decade torch nearly 2000 homes and destroy billions of dollars of real property, while other heat-related aberrations left over 20,000 dead in Italy, France, and Portugal, in the worst heat-wave and wildfires to strike Southern Europe in a generation. The annual parade of hurricanes through the Caribbean Sea, South Atlantic Ocean, and the Gulf of Mexico has seen seven of the ten most disastrous hurricanes

---

[29] By 2020, 5 of the 6 most devastating wildfires in California's history will occur in the 2020 fire season.

in history present during the past five years, with four of them bitch-slapping Florida and the Gulf Coast last year alone.

Hurricane Katrina brings this week a new measure of the distance between things, and whether one believes it's an expression of "intelligent design," or of "some vast conspiracy," the effect of "global warming," or even of something we have nothing to do with, and can do nothing about—it's worth noting a few things:

The Earth is Alive. An earthquake of magnitude 5.0 or more is recorded somewhere on earth over 1,300 times a year, and a wealth of information and data points to our planet's throbbing core.

Little of what mankind does on earth will have much of an effect, in the end. The powers, forces, and changes of NATURE will trump our brilliance, and planning, and effort every time. Our relentless pursuit of progress and profit may indeed have the effect of rendering the earth's natural forces more ferocious and destructive; or perhaps those skeptical of science are correct, and man's designs are inconsequential. Either way, Mother Earth will have the final say.

That certainty, should it have been debatable for any reason prior to this past Monday and Tuesday, ought now be clear in the face of what has become of New Orleans and nearby parts of the Gulf Coast.

Can anyone doubt the Earth will reclaim Louisiana's swamps and wetlands in her own time and manner?

For good reason do the cultures of people with the longest histories on our planet feature knowledge, ritual, and celebration of living in harmony with the forces and elements of Nature. As a relatively short-lived people ourselves, we Americans would do well to seek a greater measure of that kind of harmony, and soon, if we wish to keep spreading our way of life all over the globe.

It is also worth noting that the Bush administration, with typical wrongheadedness, malfeasance, and poor timing, recently gutted the budget for the New Orleans District of the Army Corps of Engineers, almost certainly making what would have been a bad situation in any event, even worse.

One may also rightly consider the possibility that, had not the vast majority of our National Guard been deployed on a fool's errand in Iraq, the chaos, looting, and mayhem that have plagued New Orleans in Katrina's wake might have been diminished.

September 7

As floodwaters begin to recede from New Orleans, the bloated, rotting corpses of thousands of Hurricane Katrina's most obvious victims are not the only ghastly elements of the disaster surfacing.

For any who care—nay, dare—to look, the callousness, megalomania, and utter incompetence of the Bush Administration has also shown itself in all its criminal wretchedness. And while Karl Rove and a host of the nation's genteel lawmakers have decreed that what happened in the City that Care Forgot during the past week was either the fault of local politicians, or nothing for which anyone should point fingers in blame, the truth of the matter is that the President should turn in his scorecard and head for the 19th hole.

The State of Louisiana has a long, proud history of taking its statehood in our republic quite seriously. It stands alone, perhaps, in transcending the onslaught of fast food chains, big lot supercenters, and branded consumerism that renders such homogeneity to so many of our blessed United States.

Since before the founding of the nation, Louisiana has nourished and preserved—and neglected and poisoned—a culture at once connected to and distinct from anything one thinks of today as American.

No city outside New York or Los Angeles can match New Orleans in any matrix counting cuisine, music, eccentricity, debauchery, danger, and style.

But none of that—leaving aside the actual poor, black, drug-addled lowlifes, misfits, old people, and helpless children who suffered and perished with Katrina—none of the real interests at stake mattered to George W. Bush when time came to act.

One presumes he himself had little understanding of the matter, and was more than happy to play golf when Mr. Rove and Mr. Cheney said it would be fine, but Mr. Bush ought to be held accountable anyway, for holding New Orleans and Louisiana hostage to a policy of abdicating all responsibility outside absolute fealty to federal control.

Louisiana Governor Kathleen Blanco declared a state of emergency three days before the hurricane made landfall and was presented by White House lawyers (our future John Robertses) with a take-it-or-leave-it proposition that would have had her abdicate immediate and total control of state and local authority to the federal government. She demurred, and Dubya teed it up.

That was fine with him, since his administration had been long-gone from the disaster response business anyway.

Mr. Bush took a cabinet-level position with its own distinct mission and a stellar record of having shown the country its best intentions and brightest ideas after events like the Midwestern floods of '93, the Northridge earthquake of '94, and the Oklahoma City bombing of '95, and folded it into the massive bureaucracy of the Department of Homeland Security. He reduced the Directorship of the Federal Emergency Management Agency to a position fit for a man who failed to effectively manage a horse breeding association, and was known around the White House as "Brownie."

Now comes Mississippi Republican Senator Trent Lott, saying things are "never perfect after a natural disaster," graciously ceding his antebellum home in Pascagoula, MS, for the team.

John Cornyn, the Republican from Texas says, "The last thing we need to do is to drag the secretary of Homeland Security and the director of FEMA in."

Mel Martinez, Republican of Florida, allows "There will be plenty of time...to pick over the bones," and the Republican from Montana, Conrad Burns, reminds us "We are burning a lot of money down there, we are going to ask for a little more accountability for how that money is being spent and where it is going."

While this administration has spent hundreds of billions of dollars in the last several years fomenting terrorism and anti-American sentiment abroad, real live Americans have been ignored and short-changed at home.

Now we've exposed our willingness to sacrifice our most vulnerable, discount our most unique, and extort our most damaged in pursuit of some caricature of a God-fearing, sober Soldier of Good in the War Against Evil.

Mr. Bush has turned a federal government that once prepared to defend its citizens into one prepared now only to dominate or abandon them.

2006

January 19

The White House has reached the denial phase in its twelve-step journey toward creating a better place for us all.

Press Secretary Scott McClellan today professed a complete lack of knowledge of U.S. government-ordered and executed renditions of private citizens to places like Syria and Egypt—where the loosest standards of tortuous interrogation routinely apply.

Told by reporters that U.S. renditions to Syria had been "well publicized," McClellan sneered, "What, by bloggers?"

In fact, stories about U.S. renditions to Syria have been published by the Washington Post, the New York Times, the Associated Press and the New Yorker. The president's widely known eschewal of printed matter appears to have infected even his own liaison to the press.

Among other liaisons, embattled Republican Senator Rick Santorum, not long ago one of his party's leading lights and one of its most aggressive proselytizers for a new morality, came down with an epic case of amnesia this week when confronted with boastful things he once said about the now-disgraced Jack Abramoff and his personal backdoor route to Congress, "K Street."

"I don't know what you mean by Senate liaison to the quote, 'K Street Project,'" Santorum told reporters Tuesday. "I'm not aware of any Senate liaison job that I do for the K Street Project."

Mr. Santorum has been joined by droves of Republicans on Capitol Hill seeking to wish memory of their dealings with Mr. Abramoff into the cornfield. While the spin has been to try and describe Mr. Abramoff as an equal-opportunity fixer, he himself gave direct cash contributions exclusively to Republicans, and the entire body of his lobbying "work" was in service of Republican interests and Republican causes.[30]

The stench of fear runs all the way to the carpeted hallways of the White House.

Asked last week if the executive branch would be making available logs of Mr. Abramoff's comings and goings in the White House, Mr. McClellan promised reporters a "thorough report." Released on Tuesday, the report was that, during Mr. Bush's tenure as the nation's chief executive, Mr. Abramoff has attended two Hanukkah parties and an unnamed number of "staff-level" meetings.

Mr. McClellan declined to address questions as to who else attended such meetings and what subjects were discussed, but he reassured the nation that "if you bring something to my attention ... I'll be glad to look into it. If you've got something specific, I'll be glad to take a look into it."

Asked pointedly if Mr. Abramoff had met with presidential cornerman Karl Rove, Mr. McClellan averred, "We don't—we don't ever tend to get into those staff-level meetings."

---

[30] Jack Abramoff is an American lobbyist, businessman, movie producer, writer, and convicted felon. He was at the center of an extensive corruption investigation that resulted in his conviction and to 21 people either pleading guilty or being found guilty, including White House officials, a U.S. Representative, and nine other lobbyists and congressional aides. After a guilty plea in January 2006, he was sentenced to six years in federal prison for mail fraud, conspiracy to bribe public officials, and tax evasion.

March 19

On the third anniversary of the United States' commencement of hostilities in Iraq, the government's top three executives—President George W. Bush, Vice President Dick Cheney, and Secretary of Defense Donald Rumsfeld—today asked a watching world to suspend belief in reality and accept the notion that War is Peace.[31]

Confronted on the CBS news program Face the Nation with his statement three years ago that American troops would be "greeted as liberators" in Iraq, and with his assurance ten months ago that the insurgency there was "in its last throes," Mr. Cheney said his statements were "basically accurate" and blamed the news media for creating a different "perception" by reporting on the daily litany of death and destruction that have plagued the nation since American troops stage-managed the toppling of Saddam Hussein's statue in a Baghdad square three weeks after the invasion.

Mr. Cheney sought to distance himself from the inaccuracy of his previous statements about the war by looking to the future. "It's not just about Iraq, it's not about just today's situation in Iraq," he said. "It's about where we're going to be ten years from now in the Middle East and whether or not there's going to be hope and the development of the governments that are responsive to the will of the people, that are not a threat to anyone, that are not safe havens for terror or manufacturers of weapons of mass destruction."[32]

---

[31] "War is Peace" is perhaps the most famous example of doublespeak, a concept itself made famous by the author George Orwell in his seminal novel about government and society, 1984. The George W. Bush era in American politics was often referred to by people and by some in the media as "Orwellian."

[32] Fourteen years later, over 80,000 US military personnel remain stationed in the Middle East region, with about a quarter of them engaged in active conflicts in Iraq, Afghanistan, and Syria. The U.S. continues to spend nearly $1.5 billion annually on foreign aid to Iraq alone.

Right.

For his part, the architect of the American war effort, Mr. Rumsfeld, wrote in an op-ed piece published in the Washington Post that failing to see the job finished in Iraq would be akin to our having turned post-war Germany over to the Nazis after World War II, or to asking former Soviet-bloc nations to return to Soviet domination after the fall of Communism in Eastern Europe.

Let it not be said that anyone in the Bush administration is bereft of delusions of grandeur.

When the war was launched, the Pentagon expected a short conflict. Its classified plans called for the withdrawal of the majority of American troops by the fall of 2003. Today roughly 133,000 remain there on combat duty and force commanders predict that "significant numbers" of troops will be required for at least "a couple more years."

The president, who stood on a U.S. aircraft carrier in yet another stage-managed set piece in May of 2003 to declare the mission accomplished, failed to answer questions today about the disparity between his expectations three years ago and the present reality in Iraq, saying only, "I'm encouraged by the progress," before retreating to the cozy confines of the big house on Pennsylvania Avenue in the nation's capital.

Meanwhile, Ayad Allawi, the former Prime Minister of Iraq who was once hailed by Mr. Bush as the kind of fair-minded leader needed by the Iraqi people, put things rather bluntly in an interview with the BBC: "We are in civil war."

So there you have it, we're either doing a "heckuva job"[33] in Iraq, or the country is about to go into the toilet.

---

[33] "Heckuva job" origins: https://www.nbcnews.com/storyline/hurricane-katrina-anniversary/heck-job-brownie-where-disgraced-fema-head-now-n400436

For those of you keeping score at home, 2,318 American service personnel have perished in the three years of this war; 17,124 have been wounded.

Iraqi casualties remain uncounted.[34]

June 3

The U.S. Senate will begin debate next week on a constitutional amendment being pushed by President George W. Bush and the White House to define marriage as a union between a man and a woman. The proposed amendment also prohibits judges from ruling that either the Constitution or any state may give same-sex couples the right to marry or the same legal rights as married couples.

One would think people have more pressing concerns.

Nevertheless, the president used his weekly radio address today to flog the idea that the institution of marriage needs protection from "activist judges and some local officials [who] have made an aggressive attempt to redefine marriage in recent years." He'll be addressing the issue again on Monday in a nationally broadcast speech.

I can appreciate the president's wish to give Americans insight into his thinking on important matters, and no doubt the senate ought to give full and fair debate to issues of national relevance as often as its members' busy fundraising schedules will allow.

---

[34] In January of 2020, the Iraqi Prime Minister would finally demand the departure of US troops from the country after the US President ordered a drone strike on a Saudi Arabian oil field in Iraq to assassinate the beloved Iranian general, Qassem Soleimani. As of September 2020, 3,500 US troops remained in the country. The Defense Department stopped counting troop deaths in Iraq in 2011 at 4,576, with 32,222 recorded as wounded. Accurate numbers of Iraqi dead and wounded remain unknown.

But *this issue*, now?

There are dozens of reasons why this issue fails to merit consideration as something to address at the constitutional level, and it is widely acknowledged to have no chance whatsoever of being passed by Congress.[35]

So why on earth is the president bringing it up again nearly two-and-a-half years after he first proposed it?

Because he's a divider, not a uniter. The man has no observable interest in bringing the citizens of this great nation together on even a single issue of real importance.

He prefers to do most of his work in secret, as far away from public view as possible, and every time some little bit of light shines public or media attention on his criminal ineptitude or his designs on unitary executive power, he trots out something to fan the flames of fear, jingoism, and intolerance that burn beneath the veneer of our country's global preeminence.

With the lowest approval rating of any president since that other notorious criminal, Richard M. Nixon, Mr. Bush could be forgiven a craven play for a boost in his popularity. His choice of a constitutional amendment to ban gay marriage as the vehicle to rally public support only proves his tin ear and his remove from reality.

---

[35] As expected, the Bush-pushed amendment went nowhere, but that did not stop conservatives and mainly-Christian religious zealots from spending years in the courts trying to carve out exceptions to the constitutional protections guaranteed all Americans with respect to their application to gay, lesbian, and transgender citizens. In 2015, the U.S. Supreme Court would finally rule, in the landmark case Obergefell v. Hodges, that the right to marry is guaranteed to all.

He and his advisers may be betting this obvious genuflection before theoretically inclined American conservatives will bring together God-fearing Republicans and Democrats alike and prevent the Republicans from losing control of Congress in the Fall elections.

Instead, it is far more likely to galvanize clear-thinking people on both sides of the philosophical divide to neutralize the nut-job-in-chief—until a new decider can be chosen in 2008.[36]

September 5

I posted the following comment to a blog entry on this date. The blog entry was about how the U.S. could have left Iraq at that time, how the government's purportedly main objective had been accomplished, and how there was no good reason to maintain a military presence there, or even in the region. I include it here because I feel it encapsulates something imperative about my thoughts around government, society, and the essential nature of what it means to be human:

While democracy would appear to ensure most favorable conditions for its flourishing, liberty, like faith, is ultimately personal. It is in fact the complete inverse of freedom without responsibility. Each of us is responsible for our own liberty. By finding—not the lowest, but—the common denominator between us all, and protecting that, we ensure propagation of the species (bonus: not just ours!) and preservation of the environment.

---

[36] By April of 2006 a schism had developed between military professionals at the Pentagon and civilian leadership in the Bush administration, especially on the topic of Sec. of Defense Rumsfeld's fitness for the job. Refusing to bow to the generals' pressure that he dismiss Rumsfeld from his position in the wake of the rapidly escalating disaster the country's mission in Iraq had become, Bush came to his friend's defense and famously said, "I'm the decider and I decide what's best. And what's best is for Don Rumsfeld to remain."

It's not the actual Hollywood/HipHop/MickeyD/Wal-Mart culture that matters here, it's the ideas underlying each of those manifestations of liberty—which everyone (except for ideological fundamentalists) seems to agree is what the world needs now.

The people of the Middle East, when they get around to it, will manifest different institutions of liberty, just as the Russians eventually got around to, just as the Germans and the Japanese got around to fairly pronto after WWII.

As I've tried to explain elsewhere, the fact that liberty took hold when it did throughout the former Soviet Union had as much to do with the character and nature—as well as the economic circumstances—of the people in those lands as it had to do with Ronald Reagan's amping of the arms race or his talk about the "Evil Empire."

The mullahs of the Middle East will lose their power to the extent the people of the Middle East are willing to deny it to them. Neither w,[37] John McCain, Hillary Clinton, Al Gore, nor anyone else in the United States or Great Britain will alter that fact. We have much more to do here than we have to do there, in my opinion.

September 28

w came one step closer today to wielding the power to undo nearly 800 years of human progress with the stroke of a pen.

By a vote of 65–34 (Maine's Olympia Snowe could bring herself to neither a yea nor nay on the matter), the U.S. Senate approved The Military Commissions Act of 2006, which is, in the august chamber's

---

[37] 37 "w" in its lowercase form, was how I tended to refer in print to the 43rd President of the US. by this point. I did so because it was his middle initial but I used it in its diminutive form to express my diminished opinion of him as a person and as a leader.

quaint description, "a bill to authorize trial by military commission for violations of the law of war, and for other purposes."

Earlier this week, the House approved its version of the legislation, roundly acknowledged to bestow upon the executive the authority to designate certain persons to whom the legal and humanitarian concordance of the past millennium shall no longer apply.

The Writ of Habeas Corpus—a right to become informed of the charges upon which one might find oneself in a dungeon, or suspended above a pot of boiling oil, or strapped to the seat of an airliner on the way to a prison that doesn't exist, or even under house arrest, a right whose observance in the year 1215 informed the very foundation of this idea we call "civilization"—will no longer be available to some.

Articles IV, V, VI and VIII of The Bill of Rights, wherein a body's right to be free of search or seizure absent some oath or affirmation of charge; to the due process of law in deprivation of life, liberty, or property; to be confronted with witnesses against oneself and to have the assistance of counsel for one's defense; to be free of cruel and unusual punishment—all fundamental principles upon which the United States of America was founded, which have been enshrined in the fabric of our very legitimacy as a nation and a people since 1791—those will no longer apply to some.

The Rules of War, a set of conventions and "best practices" that so-called civilized nations have been dedicated to formalizing and observing since 1864, along with very specific understandings of the rights of persons captured in wartime dating from 1949—those will be observed no longer.

The buzz has to be staggering for the former pep squad member and notorious party boy. The best the old man could manage was selling out American hostages to win an election, and puking in the Japanese

Prime Minister's lap.[38] The son gets to undermine the stability and security of the entire planet.

The mother must be so proud.

December 30

As the Year of the Fire Dog prepares to trot off, wagging its oblivious tail and bearing its friendly, sloppy grin for another twelve year jaunt through the cosmos, I am making a note to leave 2018 open. Should I be graced with life the next time a Year of the Dog comes bounding into view, I believe I'll find it far more bearable with nothing too important on the schedule, as opposed to this waning year, when I've been stymied at every turn. So, goodbye Dog, and good luck.

On February 17 we welcome the Fire Pig. And, according to my favorite astrologer, the Pig wants to party.

2006 will go down as the worst year in my memory. I think back to the last Dog year, 1994, and recall certain difficulties; it was, after all, the year the Republican party took control of Congress. And the Dog

---

[38] On January 8, 1992, while attending a banquet hosted by the Prime Minister of Japan, Kiichi Miyazawa, U.S. President George H. W. Bush fainted after vomiting in Miyazawa's lap. Doctors have since attributed the incident to a case of acute gastroenteritis. The incident was widely reported, coming just weeks before the New Hampshire Primary, and quickly became fodder for comedians. Footage of the President vomiting was broadcast on the ABC network. The incident was parodied by Saturday Night Live with a mock documentary featuring Barbara Bush trying to escape by crawling across the table, itself, perhaps a vomit-inducing reference to the assassination of President John F. Kennedy in 1963. In Japan, even years later, Bush was remembered for this event. According to the Encyclopedia of political communication, "The incident caused a wave of late night television jokes and ridicule in the international community, even coining Busshu-suru (ブッシュする) which literally means 'to do the Bush thing'.

year prior to that was 1982, when the madness ushered in by Ronald Reagan was just picking up steam.

But this past year has been a horrible one for me personally and, I daresay, for my country and my planet as well.

History will remember this as the year the Commander in Chief of the United States could not recall—or decide—his course in the prosecution of the so-called War on Terror; the year in which the Executive branch of government openly proclaimed its refusal to adhere to laws regarding warrantless surveillance of U.S. citizens, in which the centuries-old right of habeas corpus was repudiated, in which science, and the environment, and truth were stifled, ignored, and manipulated—to the benefit of wealthy industrial interests who carted off billions in ill-gotten gains, laughing all the way to the bank.

We'll remember 2006 as the year a "blue ribbon" panel of dignified civil servants declared the situation in Iraq "grave and deteriorating," an assessment received by the President as a call for the commitment of additional U.S. fighting forces to the fray.

And, as of 6:00 a.m. Baghdad time on Dec. 30, we'll recall the final act in the brutal life of Saddam Hussein.

Perhaps historians will one day ponder the bitter ironies of Saddam's swift, quiet execution. A man reviled the world over as one of the most vicious tyrants to ever walk the earth, a catalyst for the expenditure of countless billions of dollars and the wasting of uncounted thousands of lives by the U.S. government, was hanged for the killing of 148 people who were detained after an attempt to assassinate him in the northern Iraqi city of Dujail in 1982. No trial or conviction on the allegations of his having gassed Iraqi Kurds, no execution on a conviction of his having been responsible for the deaths of hundreds of thousands—if not millions—of his countrymen.

Such an airing of Saddam's atrocities would have proved far too embarrassing to the Americans who made, and in the end, broke him.

As the Middle East scholar Juan Cole noted, Saddam—funded and protected by the United States when it served our leaders' interests—has thus been transformed from villain to martyr, and he may well serve as a symbol for increasing sectarian violence in the devolving chaos that now engulfs the land once known as the Cradle of Civilization.

Things could be worse.

The American electorate could have failed to wrest control of Congress from the Republican party in November's elections.

A much larger piece of the Arctic Shelf could have come undone from Ellesmere Island in the north of Canada.

Osama bin Laden could still be at large. Oh, wait. He is still at large. But it could still be worse: it could matter.

Despite personal trials and tribulations this year, I'm grateful for much. Most importantly, I reversed a nearly two-year slide into torpor and poor diet, and I am now six months into a rigorous kickboxing routine; I've begun to renew my meditation practice; and I'm playing and writing music again.

My wife and my son are both healthy and joyful; our family is loving and close-knit. I have a small circle of supportive and generous friends, and I feel no matter how dark things may seem in the world, or how desperate, I have hope and confidence in better days to come.

Happy New Year.

2007

January 3

A couple of stories had various jaws flapping today, neither of which reflects too well on the media, the punditocracy, or the so-called leadership position of the United States in world affairs.

In one, certain quarters are up in arms over the cellphone camera recording of Saddam Hussein's execution, to which I linked yesterday. In the other, presumptive 2008 Democratic presidential candidate Barack Obama is learning quickly the calculus of celebrity in the modern age.

Let's look at these seemingly unrelated stories one at a time, shall we?

With a daily death toll averaging more than 75 persons each and every over the past six months, the Iraqi government has a ways to go before it can boast of any ability to maintain order in its society (let alone deliver basic services to its citizens), but it has clearly learned a thing or two from its American enablers when it comes to political fallout.

Shit hits the fan over a poorly managed government enterprise? Call for an investigation!

In its response to the cries of foul over "unofficial" footage of Saddam's hanging, the government of Prime Minister Nouri al-Malaki actually went its BushCo counterpart one better, arresting today a government official accused of making the unauthorized recording of Saddam on the gallows. But like much of the faux due diligence that passes for self-investigation in American government circles, something about this "ExecutionGate" scandal is rotten at the core.

Saddam Hussein was hanged in a cramped room in front of about twenty-five or thirty people. Can it truly be possible the "officials" responsible for "security" at the event were somehow unaware of someone in the front row with a cellphone camera? Either the Iraqi government has absolutely no hope of ever taking even the slightest bit of control of its country—in which case we ought to get our young boys and girls the hell outta there as quickly as humanly possible—or the event managers at the hanging simply didn't care who was taking pictures.

I understand the probative value of anecdotal evidence, but I was picked out of a crowd of thousands in a darkened arena by redneck rent-a-cops in nylon windbreakers, and booted out of a ZZ Top concert in 1988, for just *holding* a camera. Perhaps Iraqi security forces are being trained by the wrong people.

Which brings us to Barack Hussein Obama, the charismatic junior Senator from Illinois, who has become the It Girl of American politics since the Democratic party's landslide sweep of November's midterm elections.

In the space of nine weeks, amid rampant speculation on all fronts as to Mr. Obama's intention to run for the Democratic nomination for President in 2008, the mainstream media has:

- called him a "flip-flopper" because he said back in 2004 he would not run in 2008, then changed his position to undecided after the November elections;
- intimated that a member of his staff had connections to an accused Illinois racketeer;

- addressed his appeal to white audiences by questioning his credibility as a black man;
- speculated on the significance and meaning of his middle name;
- shown him in split-screen on television news with images of Osama bin Laden and Saddam Hussein;
- published a television news graphic with a photograph of Osama bin Laden and the caption "Where's Obama?"; and
- finally got around to reading his autobiography, published eleven years ago, in which he admitted to using pot and cocaine in high-school, and driven the speculation meter off the charts with an inability to decide whether his candor helps or hurts his chances if he decides to run.

Honestly, the United States of America is sitting on the precipice of absolute self-immolation. And it's being led there hand-in-hand by the government and the media, the first of which has become so bloated, and so corrupt it may be beyond salvation, while the latter is so pleased with its own magnificence it's become utterly useless as a source of news and information.

The founding document says "We the People," and if we, the people, don't rise out of our collective stupor soon, we'll enjoy the same kind of freedom and democracy they have over in Iraq. We should start by doing a better job of disposing of our current leader than they did of disposing of their last one.

March 5

I am tired.

Not because I face another night of fitful sleep, anxious for my job, my seven year-old, and the pain of a strained trapezius—though there is that.

Rather, I am tired of the realization no matter how obvious it becomes, no matter how far into plain view we might drag the venality and incompetence of the Bush administration, no matter how precipitous a catastrophe to which it may lead the nation and the world, this presidency will be permitted to run its natural course.

I suppose it makes sense to retain faith in "the system" that brought us this far. We rightly ought to trust elections in 2008 will marginalize the warmongering scolds of the Bush administration and their neoconservative allies, who have abused legislative and executive prerogatives to plunder the treasury and squander the commonweal lo these many years.

Surely the republic has weathered in its brief history graft, cronyism, near-sightedness, and rapacity the equal of this administration, no? On the other hand, one wonders just how much debasement of every principle upon which the country was founded might cause "the people" to assert their power, to throw off the depredations of illegitimate, incompetent rule.

In the nearly two weeks since I mentioned Dick Cheney's incomprehensible reading of the British retreat from southern Iraq as a good thing, Bush administration support for the troops has been graphically depicted in scenes from the VA's flagship Walter Reed Army Medical Center in Northwest Washington, curiously enough, in the administration's own backyard. Small wonder the systemic rot evinced at Guantanamo, Abu Ghraib, and countless Black Sites across the globe would fester right at home among the very front-line victims of this government's hubris.

We've been treated to an explication of political moxie that cost half a dozen or more U.S. Attorneys their jobs, while donors and fixers for BushCo replaced them. The President of the National Manufacturers Association was named Chairman of the Consumer Products Safety Commission.

A high-level State Department position welcomed a man whose published work views the U.S. not as a republic, but as "a global empire," and whose entire foreign policy world view is centered around the need to maintain and expand that empire through an "imperial strategy."

At the same time, world equity markets have stumbled notably on the realization of systemic problems with the financing of the global economy; declining prices for crude oil, precious metals, and real estate indicate a contraction in core global stability. Or the tightening of the collective sphincter.

A suicide bomber got within hearing distance of Vice President Dick Cheney on his surprise visit to Afghanistan last week. Ann Coulter emitted another cloud of heinous bile at the annual Conservative Political Action Conference. The Fourth U.S. Circuit of Appeals set new limits on access to judicial redress of grievances.

On the other hand, a full and formal Bill of Indictment for Impeachment was published against Dick Cheney.

Hope springs eternal.

September 10

On January 15, 1968 the Jimi Hendrix Experience released its second album, *Axis/Bold As Love*, containing what would become the genre-defining psychedelic rock song, "If 6 Was 9."

The song was not only a statement of Mr. Hendrix's compositional innovation and his prowess on the electric guitar, but with it he also gave voice to the growing disconnect between the realities of life perceived by members of "The Establishment" and the mostly-young members of American society whose influence was then on the rise.

Today, the testimony of General David Petraeus and American Ambassador to Iraq, Ryan Crocker, before a joint session of the House Armed Services and Foreign Relations committees, marks as finished the influence once held by those who would see the world as it is.

When Hendrix sang, "Go ahead on mister businessman, you can't dress like me," implicit in his rejection of Establishment thinking was the understanding that "businessmen" are incapable of seeing the world as he did. The song also proved prescient in the lyric, "I'm the one that's gonna die when it's time for me to die," given that he was dead of a drug overdose less than three years later.

However, the independent vision and spirit that informed the song's worldview, and its refusal to "copy" the beliefs and values of then-mainstream people also helped to end the political career of Lyndon Johnson. And it served as inspiration for the waves of social and political change that swept the country and the world in the ensuing decade.

Fast-forward nearly forty years, and we can see the social and political pendulum has swung back to a point on an arc that some would argue is more regressive than the one extant in the so-called "Summer of Love."

Pundits and opinionists will disgorge torrents of verbiage—and have been doing so now, going on four years since the Bush administration committed the U.S. to war in Iraq—concerning the testimony of Mssrs. Petraeus and Crocker today. Statistics will be parsed, methodologies critiqued, goals assessed, benchmarks measured, alternative strategies weighed, and consequences pondered.

It will all be for naught. It will change nothing. It will save no one. It will neither rectify nor prevent a thing.

The United States of America has already lost the war in Iraq. The Iraqi people have yet to begin the task of forming a stable or secure or independent nation. American soldiers will continue to die in the desert for nothing (nine more died there today, most not as a result of "enemy" fire, but rather in traffic accidents).

Once the shining light of freedom and democracy, the Sweet Land of Liberty to which oppressed souls the world over looked for hope and inspiration, the United States of America is today run by torturers and war criminals who ply their deadly trade in the name of all that is good and righteous and holy.

Six is nine.

2008

January 11

The following is a reply I posted in a long comment thread/ discussion I had with a Libertarian reader of my blog. The discussion grew out of a post I'd made concerning a report from the Economic Policy Institute showing how income inequality had grown rapidly in the United States between 2003-2005.

I had made the argument that government policy choices and priorities dear to big business leaders unfairly shifted an outsized share of the fruits of technological innovation and economic output in our society to those at the top, putting undue burdens on those in the middle and leaving those at the bottom to fend for themselves. My reader, for all intents and purposes, argued that growing income inequality is the nature of things and that liberal thinking is doomed to merely wish that life be different from the way it is.

I am a middle aged man who grew up in a single-earner-income-family in the top quintile, whose parents have both been dead more than 20 years. Neither I nor my siblings bitched when our inheritance was reduced by the Estate Tax because, even though we had to split our pie four ways, we knew we were far more fortunate than the vast majority of people—and we'd have given it all away for more time in this life with the people who loved us more than anyone.

I have a post-graduate professional degree and have traveled extensively in Europe and Asia. In the mid-eighties, I lived and worked in Taiwan for nearly a year, and I traveled across Mainland China and Tibet for five months.

I have owned two of my own small businesses and provided employment to more than thirty people over the years. I have bailed employees out of jail, paid for their emergency room medical care, helped two start their own businesses, and helped one with the down payment on his family's first home in California.

I have come by my political understanding and opinions through studies in history and sociology, through my observations of and interactions with people, and by participating in government and economies on scales from the personal and local to those abstract and international.

In my experience, opportunity is plentiful and is offered without prejudice to each and every person in the first two quintiles here in America. Which doesn't mean in order to remain successful one mustn't excel in one's efforts once opportunity has been extended, though my experience has also revealed a far greater tolerance for mediocrity and laziness in the well-to-do than is generally afforded to those from the working classes.

I agree that America probably offers more opportunity for success to those in quintiles three to five than do other nations, but, in my experience, the offer comes with great prejudice and is by no means something gladly, or often enough, even willingly given by the great majority of people in the highest quintiles.

In the most general respects, my observation of this life is that, by and large, owners of property and capital are focused primarily on securing and expanding the benefits of such ownership, and any law or policy that might require the sharing or diminishment of those benefits to enhance the commonweal is met with a great gnashing of teeth.

I'll give you one specific, personal example of a tiny way in which wealth was indeed shifted to the upper 5% of income earners between

2003–2005, at the expense of the bottom 95% and in a manner having nothing to do with the mere rising up of equity markets.

My wife is a 20+ year employee of a major airline who, along with tens of thousands of her fellow employees, took a 20 percent pay cut in late 2003 as part of a corporate-wide effort to help the airline survive its reorganization in bankruptcy. The pay cut put her at the same pay-rate she had been earning in 1984 (with no adjustment for inflation). We can talk about the fundamental injustice of working at a job for 20 years and receiving average annual raises worth just over 1% in another conversation, I suppose.

After the wage concessions were finalized, the airline's CEO and several vice presidents received bonuses amounting, in aggregate, to more than $10 million, nominated of course, as "performance bonuses," ostensibly in return for productivity and efficiency gains, but as sure as you are sitting there reading these words, directly resulting from the hundreds of millions of dollars in cost savings produced by the wage cuts taken by rank-and-file employees across the country.

I can make a difference by Not choosing a leader like George Bush when I'm 18 By: Lott.

When the airline emerged from bankruptcy in 2005, three outgoing directors received multimillion dollar "golden parachute" packages and lifetime annuities worth well in excess of $100K per year. The line employees received modest stock grants in the new corporation and cash payments valued at a few thousand dollars, but continued to work for 1984 wages.

A handful of 1-percenters understand the inequities at play in our system. I can only hope they somehow manage to hold sway over the inestimable greed and sense of entitlement found in their fellow members of the rare air society because, should they not manage to do so, and fail to put in place mechanisms for shifting some of their obscene excess back down the food chain, our society may soon resemble not so much 1930s America as 1790s France.

PART 4

OPEN SALON

BLOGGING AT OPEN SALON: 2008 – 2009

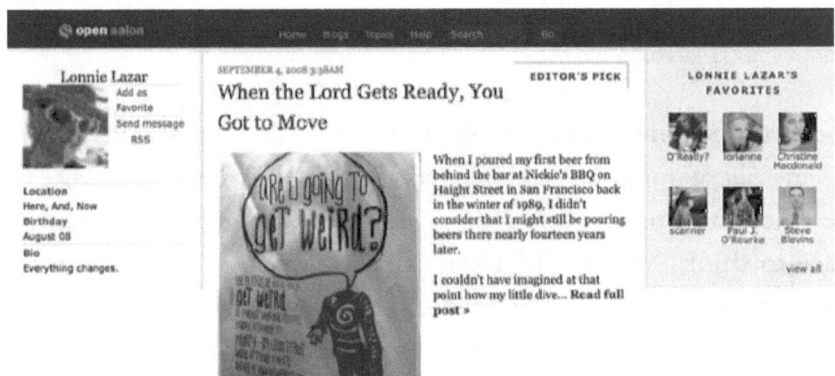

By 2007 Lofton was a 2nd grader in San Francisco's public school system. Having not worked at all from the time I sold my business in 2003 through his preschool co-op years, kindergarten, and 1st grade, I'd burned through nearly all of my savings—and Lofton's educators were less and less interested in my "parent participation" in the mechanics of day-to-day schooling.

Through a friend, I got a job running inside sales for a local Internet Service Provider. The job sucked but the pay was good, and I tried to do it well. In August the company did a round of venture capital funding and the new investors decided to clean house at the middle management level. One Thursday I was pulling in six figures and starting to think I might pull out of the debt-laden financial morass into which I'd steered my life; the next afternoon I left the office with a check for accumulated sick-pay and a "good luck to you" from the VP of Sales.

Without getting into the gore of it, within nine months, I realized my future would not feature a corporate logo.

The afternoon after I heard, "you're smart and capable but we don't think you're the right fit" for the last time, I announced to my wife, "I'm going to be a writer."

It was crazy, sure.

And it turned out to be her last straw. By the following March, we were moving out of our house and the marriage was on its way to being over, even though we moved into separate places only so she'd have time and space to think. Meanwhile, I started spending nearly all my waking hours writing for a new social media platform called *Open Salon* that was initially connected to (though quickly just loosely affiliated with) *Salon Media*, a San Francisco-based liberal publication that, at the time, was one of the most widely followed news and opinion sites on the Internet.

At *Open* I had the freedom to write whatever I wanted, and for a good two years solid I had nothing but time to do it. Thanks to the social aspects of the platform, which included the ability to "follow" and "like" and "friend" and "comment"—all of which would later become the addictive hallmarks of everything from Facebook to Instagram to Twitter to—you name it, I met some incredible people: artists, writers, photographers, musicians, poets, painters, and publishers.

Of course, none of my work at *Open* was ever paid—but think of the exposure!

My work at *Open Salon* allowed me to scratch a creative itch that had tickled more than half my life. It helped open my mind to possibilities of who I was and what I could be, and prepared me, in a very real way, for the path my life would eventually take. My first law client came to me through *Open Salon* and I met there a few of the people whom I consider today among my closest confidants, who knew me when I was at my lowest, rawest, and most vulnerable.

THERE'S ALWAYS BEEN ETHEL

EDITOR'S PICK

JULY 29, 2008

'm a guy in touch with his emotions, finally, now that I'm knocking on my fifth decade's door. But I'm not especially sentimental and I've never gone in for naming inanimate objects or anthropomorphising stuff that doesn't have a formidable quotient of sentience.

(I did spend some time in my twenties with a gal who enjoyed referring to my penis as *Elvis*, but that was her thing. Really.)

I've owned some cool cars. One, the end-of-production Triumph TR6 my father bought me in a fit of blind insanity when I was 16, in the bicentennial year of 1976. I drove it madly on the streets of Memphis and the two-lane highways of Shelby County, Tennessee, most often with the top down, wearing a leather WWI aviator's helmet, with big, round polarized goggles, and a white silk scarf tied to my neck.

Parents of some of the kids who went to my school would call our house and complain about me weaving in and out of traffic in the morning on the way to school. I tried in my own way to emulate the uber-cool of Snoopy and his Sopwith Camel.

The kindest thing you might say about that year was that it was comical. But I never named the car.

I owned a candy-apple-red 1960 MGA for twenty years, too. Lovingly restored by a British car buff in Memphis, I bought it from him in 1988 when he was down on his luck and I was flush with profits from trading commodities. In twenty years I only put the top up once, in the spring of '91, when I got caught in a freak hailstorm driving back to Memphis from the King Biscuit Blues Festival in Helena, Ark.

I eventually shipped the MG to California and spent many hours living the dream of classic motoring, up and down Highway 1, around the Bay Area, smothered in the kisses of Mother Earth among the Redwoods around Laguna Honda, over the hills and valleys and ridges of Marin, and Sonoma, and Mendocino. But I never named the car.

Only after I read Princess Dorella's[39] story of Bianca, her mannequin roommate, did I remember Ethel.

God.

Ethel was so long ago and so far away. I dare not even try to recall her as a part of my life that grows dimmer all the time, for my son quickly approaches the capability of being as stupid and wild and carefree as I was in the Days of Ethel.

---

[39]   Princess Dorella was the *nom de plume* of a favorite correspondent and fellow *Open Salon* dignitary.

Ethel was a papier-mâché sheep.

She began life as a prop in a Christmas-time manger scene on the lawn of a Hartford, CT fire station. My friend T and some buddies "liberated" her in the winter of 1976, when they were undergraduates at Fairleigh-Dickinson.

Before I met her, two years after her liberation, she had already been drinking and dancing in the nightclubs of New York City and had graced arena floors and outdoor festival grounds at dozens of Grateful Dead shows up and down the Eastern Seaboard.

T was my next-door neighbor at the first apartment after I moved out of the dorms following my freshman year in college. He and his roommate were in the Ph.D. program in Pharmacology at Tulane, where my roommate and I were undergrads. I couldn't even begin to lay out the parameters of the boundaries we crossed in those years, but Ethel was along for the whole ride.

At the apartment complex, she stood a stoic sentinel to the unhinged lust for life that was a by-product of our affection for sex, drugs, rock and roll, and for having as much fun as humanly possible.

The complex manager always seemed just a little more nervous whenever she knocked on T's door to deliver yet another resident's complaint, and caught a glimpse of Ethel perched atop a mountain of empty beer cans, or tangled in the regulator assembly of a spent nitrous-oxide tank.

Ethel was no secret. She rode with us to scenes of debauchery in the French Quarter, attended countless wee-hour sets of music at Tipitina's, was a regular attendee at the TGIF parties thrown by the Tulane Students' Association on the Quad every Friday during the Spring and Fall semesters at school.

We came to be known as *Those Guys With The Sheep.*

I have pictures, but they are deep, deep in the archives; I'm not sure I should ever put them on the internet.

I will, however, briefly relate the story of Ethel's Baaat Mitzvah.

By 1982, T, O, D, and I had all become close friends (which we remain to this day). Although we had moved on to more spread-out living situations after eventually getting evicted from that 1st apartment, we'd stayed in touch. At the start of the Spring semester of our last year at Tulane—the year D and I would graduate from college and T and O would both get their doctorates in Pharmacology—we decided we needed a definitive kick-off event, something to lead us into the Mardi Gras season, which would then give way to the jumping, swaying rhythms of our final Jazz Festival, then graduation, and our eventual departure from the City where we'd come to know each other and ourselves.

I'm not sure what magical combination of:

- three of us being Jewish;
- with friends (a couple of good ol' boys from Shreveport and Bayou LaFouche) named Pie [short for Pieface] and Billy Bob;
- who had a big ol' house on Broadway Ave., a block from campus, where we convened regularly for wing dings after they'd been duck hunting, or for big batches of Red Beans and Rice on any old Monday night (though especially during football season)—a place we called Temple Beth el Billy Bob, since his name was on the lease; and
- all of us being huge fans of the Genesis album *The Lamb Lies Down on Broadway* led us to come up with the idea of throwing a Bat Mitzvah party for Ethel—but that's what we did. Everyone wore black, except for E, who played Ethel's mother Naomi and wore a matching leopard-skin wrap and pillbox hat.

We held an actual ceremony, with blessings conferred in Hebrew upon Ethel, whose papier-mâché I had lovingly restored one afternoon the weekend prior, sitting on the levee by the Mississippi River.

It was half-a-dozen different kinds of wrong, we knew, but it turned into one of the epic bashes of our four-year stint in New Orleans. There was loud music. A house full of people. LSD and full-grain alcohol and cans of ether and plenty of citrus and sugar and starch, and a big lawn to lie down on when things got weird.

Which they did.

Late, late, 2:00, maybe 3:00 in the morning, the gathering was down to fifteen or twenty hardcores and a few strangers stumbling into the place on their own ways home. A slight winter mist began to waken some of us resting on the lawn—and Ethel was kidnapped.

Hunter Thompson wrote, "There is nothing so depraved as a man in the midst of an ether binge," and it's true.

T formed a posse. Details were sketchy and driving inadvisable, but the posse set out to retrieve Ethel. In the end, it became a simple matter of paying the ransom, which, in this particular case, was a far better alternative to calling the police.

Ethel made it through that Mardi Gras, one of the most beautiful and rocking pre-Lenten festivals of our tenure in Old New Orleans. She made it through Jazz Festival, and even graduation.

Unfortunately, her iconic reign came to an ignoble denouement at the "Rocheblave Ave. Get-Evicted Party" the following summer. When we all left New Orleans, T had given Ethel over to the care of a couple of younger acolytes in the group of many admirers she'd developed over the years.

Those fellows were over-eager in their irrational affection for an inanimate object, and left her a broken, graffiti-stained hulk, stuffed in a sheep-sized hole in a trashed, soon-to-be abandoned apartment's sheetrock wall.

Years later, I saw those pictures, too.

THE BOYS OF SUMMER

APRIL 27, 2008

With every change in Lofton's life, it seems I, too, enter a new phase. My horizons are ever-expanding and yet, with each new thing Lofton discovers, I gain a way back to my own childhood and—perhaps it's just my imagination—a chance to get things right.

This season, he's having his first experience with organized sports. He's a feisty, 2nd-grade infielder on a team of mostly 3rd-grade baseball players; one of the other dads has nicknamed him "Rooster." It's a good one, because my boy can sure scratch, and claw, and crow!

I am an assistant coach digging the opportunity to help young kids learn the fundamentals of the game. As a friend of mine put it, it's an incredible experience taking part in someone's transformation from a kid picking flowers in the outfield to a focused athlete chasing down a fly ball.

Working with 2nd and 3rd-graders, all of whom are so constantly inside their own heads, distracted and obsessed by their own shadows—on the infield, on the basepaths, at the plate—I am relearning lessons in patience. I am gaining a new understanding of the differences between the joys of participation and the pressures of competition. I am having a great time.

I FEEL THE EARTH MOVE

EDITOR'S PICK

JUNE 19, 2008

I was going through some things in the garage just yesterday and I came across the map I used on a twenty-eight day trek around Annapurna in the Nepal Himal in 1985. My friend DM and I began the trek at Dumre, elevation less than 500 feet above sea level, crossed the Thorung La pass at over 18,000 feet, and finished in the idyllic lake town of Pokhara, at around 3,000 feet.

My map has an annotation near the top center, to the right of the airstrip at Humde, is written LANDSLIDE, with an ✖ marked on the trail just outside the town of Pisang, which sits at the base of Pisang Peak, a nearly 20,000-foot high mountain of indescribable majesty. Unless you have been there, it's a fruitless exercise for me to begin to try and describe the Himalaya. And if you have been there, it's unnecessary for me to describe it, because its beauty and majesty have already been seared indelibly into your cortex. You may forget many things in life, if you are lucky, but you cannot forget the Himalaya.

The planet's youngest mountain range, the Himalaya, like all young things in this world, is in near constant motion. Its sense of life literally undulates with sound and fury, somewhere, always. Storms, terrifyingly fierce and loud, and sunshine, impossibly bright and searingly warm, come and go and sometimes stay for days on end.

Its snow capped peaks and permafrost glaciers send torrents of water cascading down boulder-strewn chasms and move incalculable hectares of earth in every season.

And yet, for centuries people have lived there, in this or that emanation of Shangri-La, and for the most part, until the latter half of the last century, they did so undisturbed by the march of progress or of demanding, hyper-competitive westerners looking to conquer the summit of each of her daunting peaks.

D and I staggered into Pisang about a half hour before sunset, having pushed hard from Chame in a single day. We'd made the haul despite gaining and losing and regaining over 2,000 vertical feet on the trail because several days before, at the prehistoric lake town of Tal, we'd been rained in for five full days, unable to make any progress in the torrential downpour and soup-thick fog. We were worried our visas could expire while we were still on the trail if we encountered additional delays, and Nepal is no place to get caught with an expired visa, for justice there is capricious and expensive.

As we settled in for some dal baht and pumpkin soup, with a side of yak butter tea at our guesthouse, we overheard an Italian guy speaking in very somber, hushed tones, and we noticed he had bandages on one of his legs and was getting about on a makeshift crutch. Delicate inquiries revealed him to have been the leader of a mountaineering expedition attempting to summit Mt. Pisang.

That afternoon, nine of the eleven members of his group had perished in a landslide a couple hours outside of town.

He said there was no warning.

His group was spread out across the wide slope of a shale-filled mountain shoulder, very much out in the open, with no trees or overhangs or any kind of embankment to seek cover under, when a low, distant rumbling suddenly turned into a shower of earthen debris. He said the sky was dark with crashing rock and most of those who died had not been buried in the landslide, but were killed by falling boulders crushing their skulls or knocking them off the trail and killing them in steep, uncontrolled falls further down the mountainside.

The next morning, as we prepared to set out for Manang, we saw the first of the dead being brought into town on stretchers carried by local porters. The expedition leader had a kind of vacant, confused look on his face, as if he had no reference point of experience from which to deal with his trip having gone wrong on such a massive scale.

D and I felt for him and thought with heavy hearts about the people on the stretchers, wrapped in burlap and yak skin coverings, how each of them had probably been, like us, young, fit, feeling invincible against the raw, challenging beauty of the mountain, relishing the moment when they might reach their summit and claim their victory on one of mountaineering's most difficult stages.

We thought of them again later in the morning, when we came to the site of the landslide, where the trail was obliterated by a sea of haphazard boulders and a tide of loose shale that made the going delicate and dangerous for us, even a full day trailing in its wake.

But we made it past the landslide with no further instabilities and crossed another half dozen or more insanely treacherous reaches of earth, on bamboo poles tied together and strewn across boulders fifty feet over raging mountain waters, clinging to mountainsides while tiptoeing on narrow footpaths with two and three hundred foot drops into boulder-filled gorges on the other side, and finally into higher-than-any-high country either of us had been in our lives, country five and six and seven thousand feet higher than the highest ski lifts we'd ever dismounted in the Rockies or the Sierras or the Alps.

When we made our summit at Thorung La, we didn't think about the dead Italian climbers; we just thought about how incredibly cold it was, how we'd never felt wind blow that hard or seen sunshine that bright. And we thought about the dal bhat and yak butter tea waiting for us in Muktinath.

BURNING DOWN THE HOUSE

EDITOR'S PICK

JUNE 28, 2008

A is an admitted pyrophiliac. As a child, he found endless amusement in setting things alight and/or blowing them up. It should come as no surprise, then, that A holds a special fondness for the 4th of July.

Every year he can be found with a cache of several hundreds of dollars worth of the most elaborate fireworks an individual can obtain legally and his home on the south side is the annual site of a pyrotechnics display that rivals those put on by some small towns. His entire neighborhood turns out to ooh and ahh, and the children, especially, love it. For many of them, it's the closest they will ever come to the red glare of rockets without joining the military.

A few years ago, A was prepared for the usual show when his beeper went off in the late afternoon. He makes his living as a product rep for a medical device manufacturer, and anytime one of their devices is implanted in a patient, he or someone from his sales team is required to attend the surgical procedure in case the doctors have questions or the operation encounters problems. On this 4th of July, A was on call so he had to leave the party, requesting his wife, his best friend, and their neighbor see to it the fireworks display got underway in the event he'd not returned by sundown.

The appointed hour arrived, along with the usual gaggle of neighborhood kids, and none were disappointed. The children's eyes danced with primeval glee as nearly thirty minutes of aerial repeaters, mortar tubes, flying spinners, fountains, mines, poppers & snaps and, of course, roman candles lit up the night sky and the street outside A's house. One of the adults, looking on at a group of six or eight middle-school-aged boys dancing and chanting around a trio of fountains shooting colorful sparks fifteen feet in the air, their faces glowing red and orange, teeth and whites of their eyes luminescent with unbridled passion, remarked to his neighbor, "It's just like Lord of the Flies, isn't it?"

When the show was over everyone pitched in to gather up the many dozens of spent canisters, tossing them all into great plastic garbage sacks, piling the sacks into A's garage before filtering back to their respective homes to revel in the afterglow of another wonderful fireworks display and drift off to sleep amid the faint pops and pows of firecrackers going off into the night in other parts of the city.

Within a half hour, the lights in A's neighbor's house across the street began to flicker before going briefly dim and finally out. The smoke alarm in A's house began to screech and his wife went downstairs to find the door to the garage too hot to touch. She ran upstairs to get their son and the two of them spilled from the front door just as two other neighbors ran up with a hammer and a hose.

Black smoke billowed from the seams of the garage door, with orange flames dancing behind its small rectangular windows. One neighbor smashed a window and the other snaked his garden hose through, hoping desperately to douse the fire before it got out of control. Soon the smoke and the heat were too much to remain near the garage and everyone retreated to the adjacent sidewalk, where the gaggle of neighbors was beginning to reconvene in stunned horror at the unfolding scene.

The fire department arrived within minutes. Soon, four trucks, a couple of ambulances and a chief's car choked the narrow streets in front and beside A's house. A swarm of firefighters hacked and shouted and sprayed at the house for what seemed like forever before the blaze was contained. Midway through the ordeal, A came walking up, a look of incredulous befuddlement on his face as he slowly realized it was his house the firefighters were struggling to save.

In the end, the flame-retardant sheetrock A had used in renovating the garage several years before, and the heavy duty fire door he'd installed at the portal to the living quarters upstairs—along with the timely response of emergency crews—not only possibly saved the lives of his wife and child, but definitely contained the damage to the garage itself.

The family lost all the papers and mementos and uncatalogued treasures many keep stored in the garage, along with their Saab station wagon and most of A's wine collection.

Though no fire damaged their living quarters upstairs, the house suffered extensive smoke and water damage throughout, and A and his family were forced to rent a home nearby for close to a year while the garage was rebuilt and modern disaster recovery techniques were applied to help them forget, on occasion, how that particular 4th of July turned into a dud.

DON'T JUST SIT THERE, DO SOMETHING

September 2, 2008

Monday was a beautiful day in the Bay Area, with crystal clear light beaming in every direction. A cloudless sky lent an impossibly blue backdrop to what many consider the most beautiful urban setting in North America, if not the world.

It was a day to be out-of-doors at one of the many nearby beaches or woodland areas. Even the Marina, Fisherman's Wharf, and the concrete ribbon known as the Embarcadero that skirts the waterfront downtown from the tourist mecca at Pier 39 to the baseball mecca at Pac Bell Park, even those monuments to urban engineering had to be showing off their finest faces on such a day as Monday.

I accepted my friend Meredith's invitation to join her in Dolores Park, a glorious setting I've mentioned before in this space, which was dappled Monday with thousands of lightly dressed, sun-screened bodies of every shape and size and hue, throwing balls and frisbees, walking dogs and chasing children, eating ice cream, and drinking beer or wine or water in a beautiful natural bowl on its northeast slope, watching the local season finale of one of the great pieces of cabaret in America.

The San Francisco Mime Troupe has been creating socially relevant theater and musical comedy since 1959, making sense of every political season's headlines in a way that is anything but silent. As I sat among my illustrated fellow citizens, surrounded by families, by same-sex couples, by mixed-race groups, and by some of my own smart and caring and giving friends, I was reminded how fortunate and wonderful is my life that I live in this place. And how fitting to watch on Labor Day, in an election year, the Mime Troupe's current production, *Red State*.

Part *Network*, part *It's a Wonderful Life*, and part *Wizard of Oz*, *Red State* tells the story of Bluebird, Kansas, where apple pie has been replaced with government cheese, general stores have made way for pawn shops, and hard work on the job has become the hard work of survival. Littered with a crumbling New Deal infrastructure, with its monuments to a feisty union past forgotten, Bluebird is ready to slip into oblivion.

As a result of a voting machine malfunction, the citizens of Bluebird find themselves at the forefront of a political fight whose outcome will decide the results in the Electoral College. Can one little town hold an entire nation's election hostage?

Should it?

Is bread in the farmhouse tonight more important than deciding who sits in the White House tomorrow?

A phenomenal score, delivered by a crack three-piece orchestra, combined blues, jazz, honky tonk, and quintessentially psychedelic sounds worthy of Frank Zappa and the Mothers of Invention at their *Freak Out!* best. I was amused and amazed by the Mime Troupe's production and how it told a close-up story that made me feel the impact of current political events in my own life, and I laughed and cheered with the rest of the crowd when the cast took its final bows.

I wish every town in America had a Mime Troupe.

THE DEATH OF HOPE

JUNE 11, 2009

I n case you missed it, the Obama administration's appointment of 6'4"
Texan "Big Ed" Whiteacre to the Chairmanship of General Motors
Tuesday was the official signal that you can now take down all your
blue and red HOPE and CHANGE and PROGRESS posters. I took
mine down a while ago; they've been rolled up in the garage since April.

The honeymoon is undeniably over. All of those nasty things the Bush
administration shamed you with for eight years, those unspeakable
degradations you thought might stop if you just laid there quietly and
endured it long enough, those criminal abuses you pretended so well
were really for your own good, pretended so well that you almost came
to believe would make you stronger and better—sorry, there's more
to come.

There may still be time to change the sheets and refill the K-Y supplies,
but Big O and Big Ed and all the rest of the nation's Big Daddies are
coming back for more, so you just sit there and look pretty now, y'hear?
It hurts a lot more if you fight it. Remember that.

Edward Whiteacre, Jr., back when he was running AT&T during the
administration of George W. Bush, claimed he didn't use a computer
or know how to text message. But he sure enough knew how to lobby
the government against net neutrality, and he sure knew how to utilize
his telecommunications near-monopoly to conspire with Bush's rogue
junta in an illegal wiretapping operation that violated the Civil Rights
of American citizens in unprecedented fashion.

Barack Obama, the candidate, said on many occasions he supported net neutrality—the idea that all internet traffic is roughly equal and that service providers should not be permitted to regulate its flow "among the tubes" based on its source or its destination or its content. Net neutrality is widely regarded as one of the 21st century's fundamental necessities for the free flow of information, a concept, which, if you'll recall, began to take off with the invention of the printing press over 600 years ago.

Barack Obama, the president, has yet to publicly announce his position on net neutrality, though it's hard to imagine Big Ed coming to him and saying something like, "Y'know Barry ol' boy, I'd be willin' to get the telecom boys to cave a lil' bit on that net neutrality deal if you could see a way to put me in the big chair up there at GM."

Actually, had it not been for the sad kabuki theater that resulted in FISA reform, something Senator Obama claimed to oppose, from which candidate Obama absented himself when it came time to count votes in the matter, had it not been for that particular session of ass-fucking which the American people were forced to endure, Whiteacre might now be pounding rocks in a day-glow jumpsuit somewhere, worrying nights about his own tender sphincter instead of getting ready to take the reins at the shell of a once-proud and mighty American manufacturing concern.[40]

And what did Big Ed have to say on the occasion of his appointment to the chairmanship of the company that once set the benchmark for the automobile industry? "I don't know anything about cars."

---

[40] FISA reform never dies, it just changes administrations.

He joins a long list of executives and, as it turns out, Texans, who don't know dick about squat except how to profit personally from the great American pastimes of hegemony and empire building.

As one of the last public figures from Texas for whom I ever had a kind feeling used to sing on Monday nights in the fall on the ABC television network, "turn out the lights...the party's over."[41]

---

[41] "Dandy" Don Meredith, a former quarterback for the Dallas Cowboys who found a post-playing career as the "color" commentator on Monday Night Football, along with Howard Cosell and Frank Gifford in the 1970s and 80s. Once the outcome of a game became clear, often after a 4th quarter turnover or score by one of the teams, Meredith would break into a badly sung rendition of Willie Nelson's song, "The Party's Over."

I HAVE BIG NEWS TO SHARE

JULY 8, 2009

When I joined Open Salon last April, I had already been unemployed since the previous August.

I had been let go one Friday afternoon from a six-figure position with a successful telecommunications company in San Francisco. I didn't love the job, but I'd gotten it after the VOIP startup I'd worked at the previous couple of years failed, and it had seemed like something I could grow into.

At the time, I had very little money in the bank, having already lost most of my savings and IRA investments being ahead of the curve with respect to pessimism about the state of the general economy. When you bet large in the stock and commodities markets, you better be able to afford to lose it all, or else have impeccable timing—but I'm not here to share with you my hard-earned wisdom about portfolio management.

My point is that, when I came to *OS*, I was already pretty fucking depressed.

And I had a dim outlook because I'd spent the previous eight months dutifully trolling Monster.com and Craigslist, sending out literally hundreds of cover letters and resumes, trying to land another six-figure position to keep my family living in the kind of lifestyle to which we'd grown accustomed over the previous decade in one of the most expensive places on the planet.

So, when I got here, I was bummed, and I had lots of time. I went through all of the stages of addiction in short order and found myself posting and commenting day and night—and my family began to feel as if they'd lost me to a virtual mistress.

I kept at the job hunting though, and even got so far as a third interview at Apple Computers, for a communications management position in the company's retail division. I would have been great at that job for a number of reasons having little to do with my appreciation for Apple products and my deep knowledge of the company's natural customer base. But Apple, along with a small handful of other major corporations that looked my way for a moment, decided I was not who they were looking for.

Lucky me.

At one point, diluting my beer with tears in a heart-to-heart session with a close friend, she helped me realize the Universe was telling me everything I needed to know about my next stage in life, and that if I'd just listen, I would understand that all the closing doors and the dead ends and the unanswered cries into the vast emptiness of an unknowing, uncaring world were signs I was free to choose my own way, to create my own destiny, and to use my natural intelligence and abilities—and the knowledge gained from forty-nine years of hard living—to cut my own path through the dense thickets of fear and uncertainty that enveloped my world in the past several years.

In a way, she helped me return to myself, because that's exactly what I'd done my entire life before getting suckered into the belief that security came from a paycheck and that if mine didn't have a fancy fucking corporate logo on it I was somehow missing the boat.

My big news is that I am now open for business.

It turns out I am a licensed counselor of law in the state of California, and have been since shortly after passing the Bar exam in 1985. I never charged anyone for legal advice because I didn't need the money at the time, and it kinda seemed like the wrong thing to do, all-and-all.

It also turns out, as of today, I am a licensed Real Estate Broker in the state of California, able to assist anyone in obtaining financing for real estate purchases, refinancing for current real estate holdings, and to assist anyone in the purchase or sale of California real estate.

Those two licenses and $3.75 will get me a Grande Mocha at Starbucks, but, in addition to the meager pay I'm able to command as a freelance writer on the subjects of computers and telecommunication technology, I am now able to hold myself out as someone who can help others navigate the dreary, byzantine, often treacherous realms of contracts, finance, and real property transactions. With my good looks and charm, it's only a matter of time before I'm rolling in the dough, I just know it.

And if you call before midnight tonight, let me know you're a Member of *Open Salon*—I can give you access to my super-secret FREAKY rate card.[42]

---

[42] Freaky Troll is the beloved sidekick of OS luminary Tequila & Donuts, now a TikTok and Instagram star in her own right. She kept a page of her own on the site. She likes Ultimate Frisbee and wearing sparkly tube tops and is an all-around kick in the pants.

DEFINING MOMENTS

OCTOBER 9, 2009

Lamentations on Truth, Justice, and the American Way

A headline in Thursday's *USA Today* spoke of President Barack Obama's "defining moment" in Afghanistan—the theater former President George W. Bush chose eight years ago to showcase for the world the United States' response to the infamous 9/11 terrorist attacks (and vowed, it should be noted, to hunt down and capture "dead or alive" Osama bin Laden).

On Friday, our freshly minted American President has now been awarded the 2009 Nobel Peace Prize. It's as if some believe all the world's ills might be cured by sheer force of will—that simply by describing Mr. Obama as a decisive leader, by calling him a man of peace, history will one day reflect it to have been so.

Have the lessons of the past eight years truly gone so thoroughly unlearned?

I'm not here to suggest the Nobel Prize committee should have nominated someone else for its peace award this year. In fact, given global trends in the quest for peace and goodwill among men, I think the committee might have made a more meaningful statement by refusing to declare a recipient for this year's prize at all, making a double or nothing offer for next year's.

But I do have thoughts on defining moments I'd like to share, and present here a brief compendium of such for the gentle reader's consideration:

On the eighth anniversary of war in Afghanistan, it may be safely said the United States' adoption of the belligerent's role in that desolate land was the unmistakably defining moment of our country's pretensions to Empire.

It was the defining moment of George W. Bush's failed presidency, a failure he and his acolytes reaffirmed many times over in succeeding years.

Following shortly after his disastrous decision to invade Afghanistan, Mr. Bush's invasion of Iraq became the defining moment of the United States' pretense to being a nation of laws.

Thereafter, revelations of our sick and twisted embrace of torture as combatants in wartime at Abu Ghraib prison defined the country's descent to the moral plane occupied by the likes of ancient barbarians, Spanish Inquisitors, and tin-pot despots throughout history.

One hesitates to beat a dead horse, but George W. Bush's choice to play a round of golf and to pretend to be able to play the guitar while the greatest natural disaster in the nation's history unfolded on the Gulf Coast in Hurricane Katrina—along with the subsequent failure of the Federal Emergency Management Administration—defined the racist, classist limitations of the United States' embrace of its calling as a government "of the people, by the people, for the people."

Even as the incompetence and criminal depredations of the Bush administration finally began to see the light of day in the waning years of its terrible reign, Nancy Pelosi's declaration that "impeachment is off the table" in the wake of the 2006 elections was a defining moment in the ultimate failure of the American experiment with democracy.

This failure has lately been further defined by the present failure of congress to enact meaningful healthcare legislation, despite overwhelming evidence of the American people's desire for a national insurance plan, and despite a Democratic supermajority in the Senate.[43]

More seriously, President Obama's failure to convene any sort of investigation of Bush administration officials—from Alberto Gonzales, to Donald Rumsfeld, to Dick Cheney, and to the former President himself—Mr. Obama's failure to seek any kind of reconciliation of the previous administration's official acts with the laws and treaties of our nation has—so far—defined the ethical and intellectual bankruptcy of our entire system of government.

While it might not be as plainly evident to many as it seems to your faithful correspondent, Mr. Obama's failure to rescind the Bush administration's policies on torture and his failure to abdicate the former administration's wars in Iraq and Afghanistan, define him not as a man of peace but as a man of cowardice.

His failures define the ultimately hollow content of his message of "Hope and Change," and they define the end stages of a once promising nation, where freedom and opportunity are in ever-more-limited supply.

---

[43] In 2011 Congress would finally manage to pass the Affordable Healthcare Act, a deeply flawed piece of legislation that did manage to extend to millions of Americans healthcare opportunities previously denied them, while gifting massive profit guarantees to the private insurance industry, thereby exacerbating the problem of runaway healthcare costs for all. And because that legislation, which would become the sole, signature, defining "success" of Mr. Obama's eight years in office, was passed by a black man, and despite the fact its most significant provisions had been adapted from draft legislation originally conceived in a conservative think tank, Republicans would spend the next decade trying to undo it.

PART 5

AND THEN IT WAS

MAY 27, 2014

So. How best to catch you up on the past five years? I could start by mentioning that US troops remain in Iraq and Afghanistan, fighting and dying for no one really knows what reason—to point out how slowly things change in the global sphere.

With you and us, however, some things have changed a great, great deal, while others remain the same.

I was driving you to school this morning. It's the last week of your time at the place where you have done your schooling since kindergarten, with many of the very same kids who started with you there nine years ago. In just two days you will participate in your commencement ceremony and, as your classmates voted you, become one of the least likely to ever return.

It hasn't been all bad. You've had a few excellent teachers who understood you and encouraged the best aspects of your personality— like your independence, your forthrightness, and your sense of justice: Ms. Laurie, Mr. Lane, Ms. Kennedy, Ms. Contreras. To a large degree, however, school has not really been your bag.

I've told a story over the years that's become pretty famous among my friends, about your first day back to school in 1st or 2nd grade. I brought you there, along with other parents who returned with their kids after the long summer break, and as you and your classmates lined up outside the classroom waiting for the teacher to open the door and let you in, you moved to the back of the line and exclaimed, "I hate school! Who's with me?"

Your classmates tittered nervously and many of the parents standing around looked horrified, while I wanted to crawl under a rock but bravely assured everyone, "That's my boy!"

Yes, and here we are, with you sporting a C in Social Studies, D+ in English, F in Algebra, and F in Science.

You're not stupid.

You don't not understand what's going on.

You just don't care.

I asked you on the way to school this morning, "What do you care about?"

"I don't know," was your answer.

Hey, you're fourteen years old. You aren't supposed to have answers. You're at a fulcrum point between childhood and adulthood, which is confusing enough, and the world today is in an incredible state of uncertainty and instability.

Global climate change is a reality still denied by far too many and yet it persists, unabated.

The civic and cultural progress made in the latter half of the 20th century is being railed against by powerful forces and many of their spokespeople are being elected to office in governments worldwide to try and turn the clock back to sometime in the 14th century.

I'm trying hard not to make the disconnects between you and me your fault. It's hard, to be honest, because you present as a person who has much more awareness and capability than an average fourteen-year-old—and I expect you to be an over-average person—but I have to realize you are just a normal kid going through the normal changes that life brings to every one of the several billion human beings on this planet.

I have to meditate and consciously direct myself to let you be you, to assume my role as your protector and provider, and yes, your guidance counselor, but ultimately, to just give you the space to become the person you are.

I try to do that with love, consciously, and with intelligence, so much as I have at my disposal. I'm not always successful.

August 23, 2016

I can't tell you how many times in the past year-and-a-half I have thought to myself I really need to update Lofton's journal. So many things are happening, have happened; so much is always going on.

Now you are definitely at a stage of life of which you will have memories, even if they may not be detailed or quite accurate (depending on when you try to access them). I want you to be able to read this writing some day and have my narrative, my impressions of what is happening now, to inform your own reflections on the life you lived in your youth. But I never seem to find or make the time.

This morning, though, it's 5:15 a.m. I've been up since 3:00 a.m.

In the past couple of years, I have found, from time to time, it can be difficult for me to sleep through the night. A few times a month, perhaps more frequently lately, I wake between 3:00 and 5:00 a.m. and simply cannot fall back to sleep because I have so much on my mind. Sometimes I lie there and allow the thoughts to flow, trying not to manage them or hold on to them in any way, concentrating on my breath, and after a while, I doze back to sleep.

Other times, that exercise is fruitless and I get out of bed to come downstairs and read until 6:00 a.m. or so, when it's time to start the day.

Today, I'll make another entry here, but what on Earth am I trying to say?

You've just started your junior year in high school and still seem uninspired by any of the teachers or much of the subject matter thrown your way. You're now smoking pot on a regular basis, which I'm trying very hard to be cool with, despite your having abandoned an agreement I thought we had; you were going to abstain until you were 18.

I guess I was unrealistic expecting you to keep that bargain, given the prevalence of weed in the culture today, and in the lack of support among your peers for choosing such a path. I think back to my own early-teen years and recall how much I smoked and drank and broke every rule, of the problems I caused for my parents through disobedience and poor choices, and I feel grateful that—so far—you seem circumspect in your getting high and you haven't had any run-ins with officialdom.

Though, too, thinking back to my own experience, my junior and senior years in high school were the most troublesome, so we may yet be in store for some hard times together.

The big news, I guess, is the shift in your attitude toward your work in the theater. This past summer you had your first paid job, a position with the San Francisco Recreation and Parks Department that placed you under your theater company director, for whom you have been a star player in a dozen productions these past five or six years.

The job seemed pretty cush from my perspective. You didn't have to be in to work until noon, and could choose to leave at 5:00 or 6:00 p.m. The pay was good, and I know you had to enjoy having some spending money at your disposal. I enjoyed going with you to the bank to help you set up your first checking account and I let you manage your funds with only as much oversight and input as you asked.

But for whatever reason, you and N seemed to reach an impasse. You soured on the idea of participating in the company's fall production of The Aadams Family, despite the fact that you seem perfectly situated for the role of Uncle Festus. We spoke about it a few times over the summer and you said you have grown tired of N's directorial and management style. You said, too, that you've lost your verve for musical theater.

I've never been one to try and force you to do something you said you didn't want to do and when my powers of oblique persuasion failed to get you to reconsider, I began the process of letting it go. I'm hugely disappointed, of course, because you have a singular talent possessed by few people I have ever seen, one that certainly none of your peers has in this area, and I think acting could be a path to opportunities for you to see the world and to know yourself in ways you might not otherwise get.

My feeling at this moment is to let it all slide for a while but to look in the meantime for workshops in comedy or improvisation to give you something besides school, and YouTube videos, and smoking pot, to keep you engaged with life and yourself. You have mentioned an interest in stand-up comedy and perhaps a turn from musical theater to something more creative, improvisational, or dramatic will help you to another level in your development.

November 24, 2017

More time gone by. More countless occasions I have beaten myself up for not turning to this journal to get down some thoughts for you. Time seems to move ever faster now.

I am told it's a feature of growing older. Which is more of a problem for me that it is for you, at the moment. And soon, if it's not quite true already, I will spend all my time feeling bad about the time I have wasted. I will grasp for just a little more of it to spend in this life with you.

In the last year plus, I never managed to find you a comedy or improv workshop—and you pushed back against the idea every time I brought it up—so it looks for now performance is not going to be your thing. I am disappointed, though only because I know you have a natural talent for it and I suspect your opposition to the idea may be rooted in fear of being successful.

The fear of success is one of the most debilitating fears people experience, and it is incredibly common. I hope you overcome that fear, if it is indeed holding you back from reaching for the stars.

I realize, too, that you now have an interior life (and exterior experiences) I know nothing about.

As it is, in the past eight years you have spent far more time with your mom than you have with me, even though during the school year you have generally spent three nights and parts of four days a week with me.

I feel like we have a good relationship, feel like we are comfortable with each other, and that you confide in me with openness and honesty. But I am plagued feeling there is a part of you I don't know—and possibly may never know. I carry guilt about that feeling that stems from the separate lives your mom and I chose to lead since you were eight or nine years old.

Which brings me back to the whole grasping-for-a-little-more-time thing.

You'll graduate from High School next year. You've managed to do well. You've stayed out of trouble and I think you've made some good friends. You seem thoughtful and perceptive, and I feel certain you carry yourself with dignity in the world. For all of that, I am grateful and proud.

Soon enough, you'll be off to college. Maybe you'll take a gap year to study acting in LA or New York. Maybe not.

But the thing is, you're on your way to adulthood and I am afraid I won't know you, really know you, unless I can manage to stay alive for another twenty-five or thirty years, to give you a chance to come back to me, to realize as an adult what it means for me to be your father.

And yes, to give me a piece of your mind about all the ways in which I failed, about all the things you wish you could have said to me but couldn't, because you were just a kid.

June 27, 2018

I was just a kid April 4, 1968, when Martin Luther King, Jr. was shot and killed in my hometown.

My family—mom, dad, my younger brother, and my baby sister—were in the dining room finishing dinner when I rushed in from the TV room to announce the news. Both my parents had grown up in the east, in Brooklyn, but they'd lived in the South long enough to know a thing or two about race relations, and were savvy enough about "the Times" to understand King's assassination would be a momentous event, that it might change everything.

Indeed, for a while, shit hit the fan. I remember National Guard troops and tanks in the streets of Memphis, saw news reports of neighborhoods aflame at home and across the nation, and recall trying to understand what it meant for a "curfew" to be in place: would I really be arrested if I went outside past sundown?

The next school year commenced in August of '68, after Bobby Kennedy's assassination, in the immediate aftermath of riots in Chicago related to the Democratic national convention there, and I was sent to a new elementary school.

PDS was private, an affiliate of the 2nd Presbyterian Church, and turned out to be way different from the Memphis City Public School I'd attended from 1st to 3rd grades. For one thing, PDS was all boys. It was also very white. And very Christian.

We had "Chapel" two days a week, on Wednesdays and Fridays, where we heard about the gospel of Jesus Christ and learned to sing venerable hymns like "Onward Christian Soldiers." The school mascot was a Crusader.

As a Jew, my coming home singing "Onward Christian Soldiers" created notable dissonance: mom and dad were pleased with my musicality, but taken quite aback by the source material.

Never a dedicated follower of rules, from time to time in my PDS days I found myself having to atone for some breach of protocol or another. Early on, before the swatting of hands with rulers and the paddling of butts with thick wooden paddles featured in the 6th-grade experience, coloring outside the lines required the copying of George Washington's Rules of Civility in longhand, sometimes on paper, sometimes on the chalkboard at the head of the classroom. Sometimes in multiples, if the offense was egregious enough.

I'll say this about my private school education (about the college preparatory school I went to after PDS as well): it taught me anyone can be a king (or queen); anyone can be a leader; anyone can save the world. But a good king or leader or savior must understand history; has to understand physics and logic, philosophy, art, and science, and religion. One who would don such a mantle successfully must understand the interconnectedness of all things and appreciate the immutable beauty of all life.

Sadly, we live in a moment when few so-called kings, leaders, and would-be saviors seem to grok that shit.

Last weekend, Sarah Huckabee Sanders, spokesperson and Press Secretary for the current President of the United States, went with a group to dine at a Washington D.C. area eatery, where she was informed by the restaurant's owner that the staff felt "uncomfortable" serving her and her party. Sanders, in her own words, "politely left" without making a stink about the situation. The Internet, as is its wont, came unglued. For days now, people on all sides of the political spectrum have felt obliged to opine on topics ranging from civility to legal and civil rights.

Many on the Left agree the restaurant owner was well within her rights to deny service to Sanders and her group; some, in fact, believe, as the owner herself stated, "there are moments in time when people need to live their convictions."

Surprisingly, opinion on the Right hews largely to a view of the restaurant's position as "despicable and outlandish," rooted in "arrogance and hypocrisy." I say surprisingly, of course, because many on the Right cheered deliriously when the Supreme Court recently ruled it's just fine for a baker to refuse baking a wedding cake for a gay customer.[44]

Young denizens of Washington, DC employed in the current administration have also recently been heard to complain about the difficulty of getting dates once the source of their paychecks becomes known. (After all, a not-inconsiderable number of people out there believe the President is the second coming of Adolf Hitler, that his ascension to power reflects a paranoid, xenophobic, racist intolerance in the body politic, and that, as one person in my Twitter feed put it, "the least you can do is refuse to fuck these people.")

It seems safe to say the U.S. today is a divided nation. The President won office despite having lost the popular vote by a count of some three million; the priorities and beliefs of urban citizens are often diametrically opposed to those of people who live in more rural areas. Polls indicate a strong majority favors stricter regulation of the sale and use of firearms and yet the National Rifle Association and advocates of the primacy of the 2nd Amendment's "right to bear arms" clause perpetually convince legislators to do nothing. Many Americans believe the greatest existential threat to the country lies in "illegal"

---

[44]   The court decided *Masterpiece Cakeshop v. Colorado Civil Rights Commission* 7-2 on narrow grounds, accepting at face value the owner's claim that he refused to bake the cake for religious reasons, affirming the 1st Amendment's prohibition of government regulation of the free exercise of religion.

immigration, while others see the government's efforts to meet that threat as immoral and inhumane.

Are things worse now than they've ever been?

The head of the executive branch today routinely refers to the Press as "the enemy of the people;" he publicly belittles members of the legislative branch as "extraordinarily low IQ," "lyin'," "low-energy," and "crooked."

A year ago, supporters of the president turned out for a demonstration in Charlottesville, VA, with pitchforks and torches; the next day, at a counter-demonstration, a pissed-off dude drove his car into a crowd of people, killing an innocent young woman.[45]

At the turn of the last century though, as American workers organized and protested against the worst excesses of the Industrialist class, people died at the hands of those opposed to organized labor. In the tumult of the 1960s and 1970s, anti-war partisans bombed ROTC facilities; soldiers in the National Guard gunned down innocent students on a college campus.

As has already been referenced, in 1968 alone, a civil rights leader and a candidate for president were both assassinated, and the mayor of Chicago unleashed his police force in a bloody quest to repel largely peaceful demonstrators opposed to the Vietnam War.

---

[45]   The Charlottesville car attack occured on August 12, 2017, when James Alex Fields Jr. deliberately drove his car into a crowd of people who had been peacefully protesting a rally in Charlottesville, Virginia, killing one and injuring 19. Fields had previously espoused neo-Nazi and white supremacist beliefs. He was convicted in a state court of hit and run, the first-degree murder of 32-year-old Heather Heyer, and eight counts of malicious wounding, and was sentenced to life in prison with an additional 419 years in July 2019.

On balance, as divided and oppositional as the so-called Left and the so-called Right appear to be today, things are more civil than they have been at previous times of national division and unrest.

Not that that is necessarily a good thing.

2020

January 20

So much time gone.

Full and rich time, to be sure, but also mundane and wasted? That part, I'm not so sure about.

For the past year-and-half or so, I have had an app called *We Croak* on my phone. At five random times during the day, it gives me a notification, a reminder that I am going to die.

Buddhist philosophy holds that the more we contemplate our mortality while alive, the happier we are while living—and the easier it becomes to die when the time arrives.

Your mileage may vary.

We Croak's reminder is accompanied by a quote from some noted person speaking to the ineffable nature of this precious life. Many quotes allude to and sometimes directly address the tragedy of wasting time. Two certainties that bind each and every one of us are: we are all going to die; and none of us knows when or how. Therefore, with such knowledge and understanding, who in their right mind would fail to make the most of every moment of every day—to live life to its fullest?

To not waste time.

This calculus is not simple. For example, as I write here on a Monday morning, I have two trust portfolios and a breach of contract complaint I could and perhaps should be working on.

I am an attorney. This is a workday. People pay me to do what I am choosing to not do in favor of making this journal entry.

This particular Monday, on the other hand, is also 2020's official Martin Luther King, Jr. holiday. Banks, markets, courthouses, and federal offices of all kinds are closed in observance of MLK's birthday (1/15/1929).

Am I wasting time by writing in your journal at the expense of expending effort on things for which I would otherwise get paid? Do we waste time doing things we love at the expense of things for which we are responsible?

I don't know that I have an answer, beyond the reality that I choose to keep typing here.

I wish you luck and greater clarity on the question, in the event you choose to grapple with the problem.

I write here today, of all other days in the past nearly two years, for a couple of what I find good reasons.

First, over the weekend, I received notice from the court that your mom's and my divorce is now final. We stayed married, to be honest, because her health insurance plan allowed me to keep affordable health insurance as long as we were on the books as a married couple. Given the bicycle accident I suffered in 2015 (4 days in the hospital, 5 broken ribs, punctured lung), it was a good thing to have kept access to a decent health plan and I'm happy to have been able to pay for it over the years. But now, more than ten years after separating, we are legally divorced.

These days, especially, you spend more time on Bennington Street than you do on Gates Street. Your stuff is there. Mainly your PlayStation, I'm sure, but also most of your wardrobe; and I believe your sense of center—of home—is there.

Your mom has always had more family. I think it's one of the things that drew me to her, given the fractured and limited scope of my clan. You have over the years traveled regularly to Memphis to visit with her family and you have experience and relationships with your aunts and uncles and cousins and grandmother on that side that are totally inaccessible to me. So, I feel it's natural and fine that you are more in tune with home at your mom's place.

Of course, I long for confirmation that you feel as close to and as "at home" with me but I have been coming to terms with a fractured and limited scope of "family" my entire life.

I write today, as well, because tomorrow begins the Senate trial of the Impeachment of the 45th President of the United States of America. This is a historical moment. A fulcrum moment, not only in the history of this country but in the history of mankind, in the history of Life on Earth.

The development of civilization has been pointing to this moment at least since the signing of the Magna Carta in 1215. (OK, Western Civ-centric, I know, but stay with me here.)

On the line, in my view, is nothing less than a victory in the battle between Good and Evil. You'll have access to the historical record (even if you're not paying close attention now) but let me state with uncompromising conviction, my belief that Donald Trump is, far and away, the most corrupt, self-serving, incompetent, immoral, and utterly criminal person to ever hold the office he has now degraded for three years.

The politics of it all, and the chaotic insanity of the forces he has unleashed in Congress, in the media, and in the population, make it hard to say whether he will be convicted and removed from office as he should be.

I, of course, remain optimistic that he will not only be convicted and removed, but that he will also be tried and convicted in courts of law for multiple crimes, and that he will die in prison—an example for future generations that greed and hubris and unfounded self-regard may be punished in this lifetime.

One way or another, we croak.

July 18

Getting ready to head to the Mendocino coast tomorrow for a three-day writing retreat, where I will try and put the finishing touches on the main content for this project.

The last five years or so have meant a move to mobile computing, for the most part, given that most of my computing needs consist now of text and email communications—mostly short, grammatically unimportant and rarely proofread bursts of this or that time-sensitive thing—along with internet-based browsing of news, information, and the occasionally prurient scrolling of imagery.

Almost all of my drafting of legal documents and other long-form, considered writing I still do at my desktop—but I'm definitely not planning to haul my iMac with me in the back of the pick-up tomorrow. And therein lies a bit of a rub: long-form writing on an iPad has improved by many leaps and bounds in the past five years, but it remains a far cry from the satisfying, easily amended experience of writing on a real desk- or laptop computer.

So, I've been concerned about how to manage my workflow in Mendocino.

Then I remembered I still have my 2006 PowerBook G4 sitting under a pile of something, somewhere in a closet, or down in the garage. I recalled how much of this project was conceived and produced on that machine and I thought it could be the answer.

But really, come on. A sixteen-year-old device that hasn't been fired up in nearly eight years? Would I even remember the admin password? Could it still connect to the internet?

Lo and behold, I was able to locate, with almost no difficulty, the cute, little snub-nosed marvel, a device some might argue embodies the apotheosis of Apple design. I had to root around a little longer to find the power cord but find it I did and fuck me if this thing doesn't rock and roll like I remember.

Can't wait to head North now.

July 19   Just North of Fort Bragg, CA

And here I am. Situated in a veritable escritoire, at a small writing desk tucked into a corner of the most lovely guesthouse on a beautiful piece of property just off the majestic dunes that skirt the Pacific coastline north of Fort Bragg.

It's a three-and-a-half hour drive from the City to get here and a world away, exactly what I'd hoped to find to spend the next couple of days thinking and writing and being outside of my usual space, disengaged from my usual routines.

There is a "secret" beach nearby, accessible only at low tide, which, as fate would have it, occurs during the next couple of days between 5:00 a.m. and 8:00 a.m. So, yee-haw, up with the dawn it will be, at least tomorrow, and I'll venture forth to see what secrets lie there.

It's so quiet here. All I can hear is my tinnitus.

July 20

Today I rose at dawn and drove a couple of miles north to the beach whose hidden gems become revealed at low tide.

Great, massive rock formations sprinkled along the coast, thick at their bases with mussels and starfish and other sea creatures I can't even name. It's a sight to behold.

With the sun coming up over the tree-lined ridges east of the coast, the lighting was just enough to bring out subtle shades of blue, green, and purple in everything. Very few people out at that time of day, too; a nice bonus.

I know you are a City boy, though I don't have a sense at this point whether you feed on the frenetic energy of city life, with all its noise and motion. Whatever vibes may end up nourishing your soul in this life, I retain my hope you will have opportunities to get out into nature, to explore its many variations in all its wildness.

California is blessed with so many areas set aside from development, with truly some of the most awe-inspiring natural features on this Earth. Please go there. Alone or with friends, it doesn't matter. Whatever is going on in your life, you will understand more clearly and well with time spent in nature.

Go, and get lost, as I did this afternoon on the vast sand dunes just west of the property where I'm staying. I walked out there before noon just to see what the dunes looked like at midday. Figured I'd do a quick out to the shore and back to the guest house for more writing, or reading, or playing the guitar.

I got out there fine, hit the water break, and walked a mile and a half or so north, then turned around to come back.

It was just me and the shorebirds and the waves.

I was pretty sure I'd made note of a landmark piece of driftwood to guide my return to the little path through the woods back to the guest house and I started back the way I thought I needed to go but soon enough, I noticed I was amidst a vast expanse of sand and dunes and sea grasses.

No feature around me looked even remotely familiar. Fortunately, it was just after noon and while the day was overcast, there was no major coastal fog as can be the case here. The temperature was also neither too hot nor too cold. I was in pretty good shape to be lost. It was also not a huge issue to orient myself away from the ocean and toward the Shoreline Highway I knew runs just east of wherever I was.

So I wandered.

Thinking I could find my way back from whence I'd come if I looked a little harder at where I was, I tried following prints in the sand that seemed to indicate people had recently walked there.

After about an hour, finding myself nowhere near my path back to the guest house, I finally pulled out my phone and with a weak GPS signal available, typed in the guest house address.

No surprise, I wasn't far off—but given the terrain and the lay of the land, I couldn't get there from where I stood.

I used the map on the phone and a general sense of how the dunes situated themselves to get ever closer to a road with houses on it—even if it wasn't the road my guest house was on—and just before getting out of the dunes and into a neighborhood, I came across a hammock situated atop a majestic dune, with an expansive view of the coastline unfolding to the West.

I took the opportunity to lie in the hammock and reflect on my good fortune.

After a little rest and time in the sun, I dismounted the hammock, bounded down the dune, and trundled out to the road leading to the highway—and my guest house just a mile or so away.

Took a nice, hot shower to wash off the sand and thoughts of what being unable to make it back to the guest house might have been like. Made a pizza for lunch, then drove into "town" to mail some things at the post office and get provisions from the grocery.

I suppose I meant to use this time away from my routine to address what my editor has called "the gap."

The "Gap"—that long chunk of time between my early writings here and my re-attention to getting this effort over the, what—finish line?— goal line?—but all I've managed to do is get myself away from the locus of my routines, only to find: No matter where you go, there you are.

I'll be 60 years old in a couple of weeks and still becoming my best self. Now, in what feels more like a race against time than ever before.

We, of course, never know how much time there is, nor how much we have. Not that long ago, a person might expect thirty to forty years for a lifetime and—should humans continue to exist at all—someone born today can increasingly expect nearly 100 years to figure things out.

Should my body continue to work well enough, I'd like, I think, to live another forty years—largely because I feel I am still figuring this life and myself out—I might be a little more than halfway there.

The good news, I believe, is we can always figure things out. We can always become our better selves, that, in fact, a defining feature of humanity lies in our, we humans', capacity and drive to evolve to our highest selves.

August 8   **San Francisco**

And, BAM! You're 60.

At least I am, today. I woke up, got out of bed, took a shower, and walked up to the hill for a look around.

On the way up there, I ran into a neighbor from across the street. We chatted on the stairs and I noticed she'd gathered some recyclables someone had left sitting on the curb or along the path to the park. I thought kindly of her to know that, at 80, or almost, she cares enough for her neighborhood to pick up someone else's trash and dispose of it properly.

I continued up the hill into the still, early morning. Foggy, as is the custom in the month some call Fogust here, but not cold or wet as it might be. I scanned the scant, silvery light on the horizon of downtown buildings to the north, and Bay waters wrapping east to south, and I took a few hits of nice marijuana my friend—no lie, Herb—grew.

I'd done the very same thing on many a morning since I was 14 years old, though it had been a long time, years in fact, since I'd done a proper wake-and-bake.

I looked at my feet, as one does, and noticed a plastic spoon and a semi-crushed can of single-serving coffee lying there. I thought of my neighbor and instinctively picked them up, as I turned to walk down the hill and back to the house for coffee.

Walking toward the public garbage and recycling bins at the entrance to the park to off-load the spoon and can, I was filled with a creeping awareness of the fact that I'd just picked up a random person's trash, both pieces of which had almost certainly been in or near their mouth—and began to consider what that might mean during a pandemic to me, and to some of my best friends and family—including you—who are due here to celebrate with me today.

The tips of my fingers buzzed with dread where they touched the spoon in my left hand and the can in my right. With each step to the bins and all the way home to the handle of our front door, I withstood first the urge and then the notion of an urge to touch my own face, even if just to swipe the bangs of this pandemic hair from my eyes. I couldn't wait to get inside to wash my hands.

Mortality is quite a thing. It's never been more top of mind. Not for me nor for millions, hundreds of millions, possibly billions of others around the globe.

I got a call yesterday from a client who I had helped, along with her then-boyfriend, draft a trust a few years ago. He'd been in intensive care for a stroke the past three or four days and she had questions about their documents. Turns out they had yet to marry and their documents, or the copy she can put her hands on, remain unsigned. She texted this morning and said she and his mother are making end-of-life decisions for him this weekend.

A friend in Los Angeles just called to wish me a happy birthday and said she'd never forget my birthday again because her sister died this morning of cancer.

And the doorbell rang.

It was only 9:00 a.m.

My neighbor, whom I'd chatted with on the stairs only an hour and a half ago stood in the doorway with a big bunch of bright and beautiful sunflowers.

"Happy Birthday, Lonnie," she beamed and said, "they look like you." When I say mortality is quite a thing, I mean Life, of course, is the thing. If there's any advice I might offer from this place I find myself today, it would be to enjoy your life.

Notice what happens.

If you love someone, tell them. Be nice to those you like and be especially nice to those you believe you may not. Some people will die; you, and me, and everyone you know.

And some will bring us flowers.

FLASHBACK: APRIL 17, 2018

Life is funny. And scary and sad, sometimes. Today is Dr. Das '60th birthday. He is the first of my immediate, closest friends to complete six decades of life. His achievement marks a new milestone in my ever-increasing focus on the meaning of mortality and the preciousness of being alive.

I have known Das more than half his life now—and he's known me for more than half of mine. You'll have to speak with him about what that means to him, to learn what our friendship has been like.

All I can really tell you echoes something The Chief once told me near the end of his own all-too-short life, that ended when he was but 64:

> *If you can make one or two real friends in your lifetime, connections*
> *with people you love, with people who love you unconditionally,*
> *who you accept and who accept you in all the depth and complexity*
> *of good and bad and strong and weak and smart and stupid that*
> *human beings embody, you will have done well.*

Das is one of those people to me.

EPILOGUE

Exhale.

Unclench your jaw.

Take a deep breath—in through your nose, slowly. Feel it filling up your lungs, from the very bottom to the very top—and then hold that breath for a beat... two... three...

Now, let it go, slowly, through your mouth.

Don't be afraid to make some sound.

An entire nation has been waiting to do that for five days.

Perhaps not according to those precise directions, but the people of the United States (along with many, many other people worldwide) have been holding their breath and clenching their jaws since the national election on November 3, and are today feeling it's OK to exhale.

It took some time for the result to be clear enough to media executives for them to "call it" for the television audience, but they finally did so today. Absent the ever-present possibility that anything can happen,[46]

---

[46]   Did you have "Angry mob storms the U.S. Capitol in an attempt to disrupt the confirmation of national election results at the behest of the Loser in that election" on your Social Unrest BINGO Card?

the U.S. will have a new president and executive branch of the federal government come January.

Many breathing sighs of relief today do so because the end of Donald J. Trump's time at the helm is in sight. However, my take is that we find ourselves at more of a beginning than an end.

Not entirely unlike this book.

For Lofton, its original and perhaps primary audience, the beginning is real. With his hopefully long life ahead, the presentation of this work to Lofton comes at the end of childhood and the beginning of adulthood.

Should it come to pass that these words are among the last I share with my only child, I hope and trust I've made my views, motivations, hopes, and dreams herein sufficiently clear and entertaining enough to make my memory a blessing.

For you, other dear readers, may it spark a beginning as well: A beginning of seeing your own views, motivations, hopes, and dreams in a light more imbued with ecstasy—the stepping-outside-of-oneself-kind of ecstasy—than you may have held them in prior to getting this far.

July 8, 2024

Well, dear reader, here we are. Four and a half years after supporters of Donald J. Tump stormed the U.S. Capitol, causing untold damage and resulting in the deaths of several people in what can only be accurately described as an insurrection against the lawfully elected government of the United States, a mere month and a half since Donald J. Trump was unanimously convicted by a jury of fellow New Yorkers on 34 felony counts related to falsification of business records, fraud, and campaign finance violations in his campaign for the presidency in 2016—and that same Donald J. Trump is the Republican nominee for President of the United States in 2024's election. Much current polling suggests he may win.

We live in interesting times.

August 22, 2024

Interesting, indeed!

On July 13, a 20 year-old kook with an assault rifle fired shots at Donald Trump as he gave a campaign speech in Pennsylvania. Somehow, Mr. Trump emerged with blood on his ear and a defiant scowl on his face, while the kook was immediately shot dead by Secret Service sharpshooters stationed around the campaign stage.

Whether the blood on Mr. Trump's ear came from the graze of a bullet or from the shrapnel of shattered teleprompter glass remains unclear. Why the kook, who scaled a building to his position on its roof before opening fire, and whose suspicious nature was called to the attention of security personnel well ahead of his act of political violence, wasn't stopped from firing and killing an innocent bystander is also unclear.

Near the end of July, Joe Biden became the 1st incumbent President to decide not to run for re-election since Lyndon Johnson in 1968, and only the 2nd elected President in U.S. history not to run for re-election since Franklin Pierce in 1856.

Bowing to the pressure exerted on him by senior members of his party, by a vocal cohort of the Democratic voting public, and by the polling alluded to above, Mr. Biden chose to put Country over ego and, in the bargain, gave a shot-in-the-arm to Democrats and Independents who just a month ago were beginning to prepare for the worst effects of a 2nd Trump administration.

Now, Mr. Biden's Vice President, Kamala Harris, former Attorney General and Senator from California, is poised to become the nation's 1st woman President. Poised to be the 1st woman of color and the 1st person of South Asian descent to be elected President.

We haven't had this much excitement on the political battlements since Richard Nixon resigned in disgrace in 1974 (on the night of my 14th birthday!). And with another 10 weeks before election day, well, anything is possible.

ACKNOWLEDGMENTS

Thanks, of course, go first and foremost to Lofton, without whose arrival this work may have never come forth, at least not in the form it eventually took. He is the original inspiration, a consistent muse, my proudest achievement, and amazingly, someone I feel I still need to get to know, which motivates me to stick around.

And to Janice, Lofton's mom, and my life partner for twenty years—of whom I continue to dream and give thanks for as elegant and civilized a breakup as any I know, who has been and continues to be as loving and committed a mother to our son as I could have hoped to find.

To Denise, my friend, first law client, editor, champion, provocateur, and collaborator, who believed in me and in the value of this work, who convinced me to make it so much more than a baby journal.

Another member of my *OS* family, Lisa not only read this thing but she saw it through the eagle eyes of a first-rate galley proof reader and lovingly pointed out (made me feel better about) the steep learning curve required to become a book designer and typesetter; she gave me a second chance to make it something more beautiful to behold.

Robert and Doc, my first content readers, each provided valuable insight on the missing pieces. They challenged me to dig deeper, to be vulnerable, and honest, and to tell more than I initially felt capable of telling. And to Rob, especially, for letting me know Mr. Hatchett would have approved of the writing.

To Alicia and Cola, who took me, and Lofton, into their lives, providing a home and unconditional love when we both needed those things more than anything, for whose acceptance, encouragement, and refusal to give up on me, I will remain forever grateful.

Ashley, my "Self-care Sunday" yoga teacher, turned me on to the Mary Oliver poem, *Wild Geese,* and gave me the interpretation of the passage from *The Heart Sutra* that opens this book. And my dear friend, Chrissy, a Berkeley mom who has blossomed into a true artist before our very eyes, inspired the lyric from the Vaporizers song, *Viva Lofton,* that gives the book its title.

Speaking of Vaporizers and songs, I am honored, and my life has been immeasurably enriched over the past twenty-five years, by a connection and collaboration with talented musicians who have encouraged and supported, improved, and enlivened my songwriting—and my life— who made it possible for me to live out my rock-star dreams.

I am blessed by a close-knit group of men I have known and loved as friends, and brothers, who have been my guides, companions, and co-conspirators, my mentors, confidants, and confessors, my flag-men, wing-men, and cheerleaders for thirty and forty years on my journey. These guys have helped me define my understanding of what it is to be a man, a father, a friend—a human—and they reflect so beautifully, so honestly, so compassionately what it's like for me to be me. They have encouraged and empowered me to accept and to embrace myself. I love y'all.

And I have been so incredibly blessed by the love and support of the women in my life. Of Minnie, who first opened my eyes and my heart to life's vast possibilities; of my two mothers and my few true lovers. All the great, smart, strong women who have been my bosses, my employees, my gurus, and my friends—each of whom has been my teacher, helping me learn the lesson that the only true authority in this world is rooted in self-awareness and in self-control.

Finally, thanks absolutely go to Mr. Hatchett, who did, in fact, teach me how to write.

ABOUT THE AUTHOR

Lonnie Lazar has been writing about stuff on his mind since sometime back in the late 1960s. Much of what he's written has never been read by anyone, though a bit of it was published in a High School-era Literary Journal and, if you know how to work the Google and Wayback machines, more can be found on the Internet. This is his first book. He makes a living as a Trusts and Estate Planning attorney in Northern California.

www.ingramcontent.com/pod-product-compliance
Lightning Source LLC
Chambersburg PA
CBHW030911120626
46554CB00001B/96